ENDORSEMENTS

History is strewn with the litter of unpleasant, but often necessary, theological controversies. It is one of the means whereby truth is advanced and God's church is strengthened. Keeping the long-term view helps us through controversy, knowing that God works even this together for good. And so, before circling the wagons and dividing into smaller and smaller truth squads, perhaps we should, in an abundance of caution and respect, have a very long conversation with one another. Professor Norman Shepherd is a competent and courageous man who has demonstrated in these lectures his ability and willingness to engage in this conversation in a gracious and constructive way.

Randy Booth
Pastor, Grace Covenant Church
Nacogdoches, Texas

Though I was not privileged to sit as a young seminarian under Professor Norman Shepherd, the privilege was mine to hear him present the sequence of five lectures that birthed this book. Few Christian ministers or teachers whom I have come to know personally have as graciously suffered slanderous assaults as Professor Shepherd. It seems that wherever he goes he is preceded by the falsely attributed reputation that his teaching concerning justification subverts the gospel. This unwarranted reputation maliciously imputed to him lamentably biases many to the extent that they refuse to give him a hearing. Thomas Sowell's sage observation is apropos: "Although I am ready to defend what I have said, many people expect me to defend what others have attributed to me." I commend *The Way of Righteousness* as Professor Shepherd's careful presentation of Scripture's teaching concerning justification without a hint of polemical response to his detractors. Read what he himself has taught concerning justification and discover that he is steadfastly faithful to the gospel's message of justification as taught by Jesus, by Paul, and by James.

A. B. Caneday
Professor, New Testament Studies and Biblical Theology
Northwestern College
St. Paul, Minnesota

The "Shepherd controversy" over justification has generated a number of books, articles, and ecclesiastical studies. I have expressed a number of differences with Shepherd's formulations and with those of his opponents, and I continue to disagree with him on some matters. But I greatly respect Shepherd's knowledge of Scripture and his reliance upon it. The present volume, concise as it is, is the most developed statement on justification that Shepherd has yet made. Both critics and advocates of Shepherd's position, as well as those who are merely interested, must take this book into consideration before attempting further discussion of the matter. This book will help us all to measure our opinions on the basis of Scripture, as Shepherd insists we do.

John M. Frame
Professor, J.D. Trimble Chair of Systematic Theology
and Philosophy, Reformed Seminary
Orlando, Florida

It is my distinct pleasure to commend these studies of Professor Norman Shepherd in the highest terms. I was privileged to hear the original lectures in November of 2007, and I can attest to their exegetical acumen, theological accuracy, and the warm, devotional spirit in which they were delivered. From page one, Professor Shepherd engages the biblical text and does not hesitate to go where it leads. Regarding the issue of justification and related matters, he has allowed the Bible to speak for itself and has not shrunk back from either its explicit teaching or its implications. It is my hope that this volume will receive wide distribution and that it will be influential wherever the truth is loved and honored.

Don Garlington
New Testament Scholar
Toronto, Ontario

It is no wonder that evangelical and Reformed Christians have focused so intently on the doctrine of justification. This vital truth, found throughout the Bible, cannot be fossilized in theology or reduced to a few texts in our understanding. Norman Shepherd unveils the unity of the message of James with that of Paul and the whole of Scripture, clearly explaining and warmly applying this life-giving truth.

Ben House
Administrator, Veritas Academy and Elder, Grace Covenant Church
Texarkana, Arkansas

In this small book Norman Shepherd provides the distillation of his profound thinking about the doctrine of justification. Avoiding rabbit-trails, Shepherd sticks concisely to the fundamental issues. I highly recommend this book as a guide for the perplexed and an introduction to this important Biblical teaching.

James B. Jordan
President, Biblical Horizons Ministries
Niceville, Florida

For five hundred years, Protestants have been going to Paul to learn soteriology, and then, quietly and with considerable embarrassment, tolerating or ignoring James, the crazy uncle of the New Testament. Norman Shepherd sets out to show what happens when we start with James. It becomes clear that James only calls us to the same obedience of faith taught by Paul, Jesus, Moses, and required of Adam. Justification beginning with James is, Shepherd shows, justification indeed, for it is justification by living, active faith. Shepherd demonstrates that a soteriology from James is not, as Luther would have it, a precarious house of straw, but the house of God built with gold, and silver, and precious stones.

Peter Leithart
Dean, Graduate Studies and Senior Fellow, New St. Andrews College
Pastor, Trinity Reformed Church
Moscow, Idaho

How do sinners get right with God? What is required of us to enter into salvation at the Day of Judgment? Norman Shepherd has wrestled with these questions for decades and now presents his perspective in its most mature form. Shepherd's latest work on justification should bring needed clarity to recent Reformed debates over the nature of the gospel, faith, and works. This book puts the focus squarely where it needs to be, namely, on exegeting the key biblical texts with painstaking detail. By guiding the reader through a careful survey of the place of justification in the biblical narrative, Shepherd shows that Jesus, Paul, and James are very much on the same page when it comes to justification. Shepherd's understanding of justification weaves together eschatology, soteriology, ecclesiology, and missiology into a coherent package. No doubt, his critics will find much to disagree with, but if they read carefully, they might also learn a thing or two. I heartily recommend this short, to-the-point work for everyone who wants to be a part of current justification discussions, and, more importantly, to anyone who wants a fully biblical understanding of God's method of graciously saving sinners.

Rich Lusk
Pastor, Trinity Presbyterian Church
Birmingham, Alabama

From Day One those brought to or up in the Christian faith are taught to avoid God's Law like a plague. Into this culture, Norman Shepherd wonders out loud if there might not be a better way to live faithfully in the light of *all Scripture*, rather than only those portions that support our pet systems. For this he was greeted with this response from his dearest colleagues: "Off with your head, Shepherd. You're not fit to live."

Steve M. Schlissel
Pastor, Messiah's Covenant Community Church
Brooklyn, New York

There has been much controversy surrounding Norman Shepherd's views. Now we have a clear exegetical exposition from his own hand which details exactly what he teaches about justification. I highly recommend *The Way of Righteousness* and it is my hope that it will contribute to bringing both clarity and charity into the discussion of what it means to be justified by faith.

Cornelis Van Dam
Professor, Old Testament
Theological College of the Canadian Reformed Churches
Hamilton, Ontario

In this concise study, Professor Shepherd gives us a clear exposition of the biblical teaching of justification and in the process clearly distinguishes justification by works from justification by a living and active faith. It is an excellent contribution to our on-going discussion of this vital biblical doctrine.

Steve Wilkins
Pastor, Auburn Avenue Presbyterian Church
Monroe, Louisiana

The
WAY
of
RIGHTEOUSNESS

JUSTIFICATION
BEGINNING WITH JAMES

In the way of righteousness there is life;
along that path is immortality.
Proverbs 12:28 (NIV)

NORMAN SHEPHERD

KERYGMA
PRESS

LA GRANGE, CALIFORNIA

Primitive Truths for Postmodern Times

Kerygma Press
P. O. Box 415
Mount Hermon, California 95041
www.christianculture.com

Kerygma Press is the theological imprint of the Center for Cultural Leadership.
CCL is a non-profit Christian educational foundation devoted to influencing
Christians for effective cultural leadership — in church, the arts, education, business,
technology, science, and other realms of contemporary culture

Printed in the United States of America

ISBN 978-0-578-01382-4

In thankful remembrance of

Connie Shepherd (nee Vanden Bosch)

My loving and faithful marriage covenant partner
for thirty-two years

Table of Contents

Norman Shepherd on Justification by Faith Alone: A Foreword

P. Andrew Sandlin

This is a book about justification, and the author, Norman
Shepherd, long-time professor at Westminster Theological
Seminary (Philadelphia) and pastor in the Christian Reformed
Church, writes from a distinctly and unapologetically Reformed
perspective. Heinrich Heppe, in his definitive compilation of tra-
ditional Reformed theology (1861), declares, and then labors to
demonstrate, that "the whole evangelical [i.e., Reformed] doctrine of salvation stands or falls with the doctrine of justification,
as being the inmost core of the doctrine of redemption."[1] This
language is reminiscent of Martin Luther and the Lutherans, for
whom justification is the doctrine by which the church stands or
falls,[2] and it mirrors the sentiment of John Calvin, for whom this
doctrine is the "principal hinge of religion."[3]

Shepherd stands squarely in the broad stream of this tradition by arguing (in chapter one of the present volume) that

> Justification is a judgment declared by one who is compe-
> tent to judge. Justification is a divine declaration concerning
> the sinner. Justification is not the moral transformation of
> the sinner and differs in this respect from regeneration and
> sanctification. Justification is not an act of regeneration or
> a process of sanctification. Justification is a judgment con-
> ceived and passed on the sinner by the Lord God.

---

1. Heinrich Heppe, *Reformed Dogmatics* (Grand Rapids: Baker, 1978), 543..
2. Alister McGrath, *Iustitia Dei* (Cambridge, England: University Press, 1986),
2:193, n. 3.
3. McGrath, *Iustitia Dei*, 36.

With this bold stroke, Shepherd distinguishes his views from those of Rome, Byzantium, Protestant liberalism, and many other prominent non-Reformed conceptions of justification, including sectors of modern evangelicalism. He goes on to affirm the imputation of Christ's righteousness: His righteous, atoning death and resurrection are imputed (credited) to the believing sinner's account as righteousness. In previous writings, Shepherd made plain, again in harmony with the unanimous Reformed testimony, that the "instrument" of justification (i.e., the divinely dictated action by which sinners appropriate the gift of justification) is faith alone, not works.[4] Justification is a gift of God, and it is not obtained by man's virtues, merits or achievements. Even the faith that man exercises is a gift from God, so that man may never boast of his salvation (Eph. 2:8-9).

The question that Shepherd wishes to bring into sharper focus is not, then, "What is the 'ground' of justification?" The answer by all Reformed accounts is, "The redemptive obedience of Jesus Christ."[5] Nor is the pressing question, "What is the 'instrument'[6] of justification?" The answer that all affirm is "Faith and faith alone." The pertinent question, rather, is, "What is the *nature* of the faith that is the exclusive instrument of justification?" The present work is an exploration and elucidation of the meaning of (to employ theological language) "saving faith" as it relates to justification. *What kind of faith justifies?* According to Shepherd, the faith that justifies is a submissive, penitent, obedient faith — which has nothing whatever to do with man's merit, virtue or performance to curry God's reward. Faith alone justifies, but that faith is active in hanging onto the promises of God in Jesus Christ and in

4. Norman Shepherd, "Faith and Faithfulness," in ed., P. Andrew Sandlin, *A Faith That Is Never Alone* (La Grange, California: Kerygma Press, 2007), 62.
5. There is dispute over whether the so-called "active" obedience of Christ, His law-keeping life, is, in addition to the "passive" obedience of His death and resurrection, imputed to believing sinners, but there is no dispute that Jesus' redemptive work *alone* is the "ground" of justification. But see the following footnote.
6. Shepherd is not fond of terms like "ground" and "instrument," which he identifies as scholastic distinctions; I am using them here because they are common theological currency whose meaning is generally understood.

submitting to His will.[7] For this reason Shepherd, like Reformed
New Testament theologian Herman Ridderbos, argues that faith
and works are harmonious in God's plan for man *except* in the matter of human achievement as the basis on which one is justified.
Ridderbos writes:

> [T]he contrast "faith" and "works," as we have met with
> it in such an absolute sense, is not to be understood in any
> other way than as a contrast between the grace of God on
> the one hand and human achievement as the ground for
> justification on the other. That faith and works, however,
> are mutually exclusive only in this sense, but for the rest,
> where meritoriousness is not in question, belong inseparably
> together, is evident from the whole of Paul's teaching.[8]

This construction of the relation between justification, faith
and works is important for at least three reasons. First, the Bible
warns that not all professions of Christian faith are valid (Mt.
25:31-46); not all exercises of belief are authentic (Heb. 10:38-39).
The Christian is called to assure that his faith is genuine and not
spurious (2 Pet. 1:10), and the Christian minister is charged to direct His flock, as well as the unbelievers with whom he comes into
contact, to a faith that culminates in eternal life and not in eternal
condemnation (1 Tim. 4:14-16; Tit. 1:9-16; Heb. 13:17). There is
perhaps no greater tragedy in the human condition than reliance
on a spurious belief, which in the Final Judgment will avail nothing
before God. This is self-deception of the gravest sort.

Second, Shepherd's question tests the harmony of Biblical
teaching. A casual reading of the Epistle of James, for example,
has led many to assume that his defense of justification by works
and not by faith alone conflicts baldly with Paul's stress that justification is by faith and *not* by works. Luther's infamous verdict
that James, in alleged conflict with Paul's writings, is an "epistle

---

7. This was also the position of Shepherd's predecessor and theological mentor at
Westminster Theological Seminary, John Murray, expressed in *Redemption Accomplished
and Applied* (Grand Rapids: Eerdmans, 1955), 113-116.
8. Herman Ridderbos, *Paul* (Grand Rapids: Eerdmans, 1975), 179.

of straw" has broadened out over time into a general discussion
over the theological compatibility of the various Biblical authors,
even the authors of the New Testament. For the last few genera-
tions, the theological guild has been occupied by issues relating
to the unity of the Biblical message(s). In short: do the Biblical
writers, at root, present a single harmonious message with diverse
emphases, or is the Bible a collection of ultimately heterogeneous
and irreconcilable writings that happen to have been collected into
and transmitted as a single volume? Has the Bible one message or
many messages?[9]

Third, the question Shepherd attempts to answer has momentous pastoral implications. Everybody that reads the Bible
knows (or should know) that salvation is a gift of God's grace. But
they equally know that God demands good works of His people.
What is the relation between God's grace and man's works? Does
God expect man, as the Church of Rome teaches, to prepare himself for divine grace by performing imperfect but sincere works
with which God cooperates in subsequently bringing the sinner, via
the sacramental system of the church, into a state of justification
at the end of his days?[10] Alternatively, are good works desirable
but optional in God's plan for believers, as many dispensationalists
have taught?[11] Do good works *prepare* the sinner for justification?
Do good works necessarily *flow out* of justification? Do good works
merit God's favor? Do good works *cooperate* with saving faith? Are
good works an *aspect* of faith? These are not ivory-tower theological ruminations. They have momentous implications for how the
church and its ministers preach the Gospel and lead the flock into
the pastures of Christian fidelity and, in the end, eternal blessedness. The issues Shepherd is addressing are fundamental both to
the being and the well being of the church. At some point in
church life, these issues are unavoidable.

---

9. For a recent answer, see James D. G. Dunn, *Unity and Diversity in the New Testament*
(London: SCM Press, 2006, third edition).
10. *Catechism of the Catholic Church* (Washington, D. C.: United States Catholic Conference [*Libreria Editrice Vaticana*], 1994, 2nd edition), 481-487.
11. Zane Hodges, *Absolutely Free!* (Grand Rapids: Zondervan, 1989), 73.

The chapters of this book were originally delivered at a conference in Chicago, November 2007, and co-sponsored by ACT 3 (Dr. John H. Armstrong, Founder and President) and the Center for Cultural Leadership (of which Kerygma Press is the theological imprint). It is hoped that the camaraderie exhibited at that conference, including the gracious spirit animating the discussion between both sympathizers and critics of Shepherd's views, will persist in the dialogue that the wider dissemination of those lectures is certain to generate.

Though Shepherd has set forth his position on justification and related issues in numerous places previously, the present work, while brief, constitutes a succinct and definitive summary of his views on this much-controverted topic.

I am grateful to Dr. John Armstrong and to ACT 3 for gracious permission to publish these important lectures under the Kerygma Press imprint. John's tireless advocacy of orthodox ecumenism has been an inspiration to my own life and that of many others.[12]

I am thankful also to Dave Mack for his painstaking editorial efforts. The effects of his fastidious labors are evident throughout.

It is my hope that this work will spawn a dialogue that will not become an end in itself but that will spur its readers to greater faith and obedience to Jesus Christ as Savior and Lord of the universe.

P. Andrew Sandlin (B. A., University of the State of New York; M. A., University of South Africa; S. T. D., Juan Calvino Theological Seminary) is president of the Center for Cultural Leadership; preacher at Church of the King-Santa Cruz, California; theological consultant of ACT 3 Ministries; and De Yong Distinguished Visiting Professor of Culture and Theology, Edinburg Theological Seminary. He has written many essays and articles and several books, the latest of which is *Dead Orthodoxy or Living Heresy?* He is also editing an impending *festschrift* for Professor Shepherd entitled *Obedient Faith*. He is married and has five adult children and three grandchildren.

---

12. See, for example, his "Is There Hope for the Church?", *ACT 3 Viewpoint*, January/February 2009, 1-2 and his *Your Church Is Too Small* (Grand Rapids: Zondervan, forthcoming).

CHAPTER 1

Justification According to James

There is no question more practical and more pressing than this one: "What will happen to me in the Day of Judgment?" The Bible tells us, "[W]e must all appear before the judgment seat of Christ, that each one may receive what is due him for the things done while in the body, whether good or bad" (2 Cor. 5:10). The Bible also tells us that we have sinned against God and therefore deserve condemnation and death (Rom. 3:23; 6:23). It would appear that there is no escape and that eternal condemnation is the destiny that awaits every one of us. But God gave us the Bible to reveal the gospel, the good news that there is an escape from sin and all its consequences including condemnation and death. Yes, Romans 6:23 tells us that the wages of sin is death, but it also tells us that the gift of God is eternal life through Jesus Christ our Lord.

Eternal life is a gift in the fullest sense of the word. It is not something that anyone can achieve, earn, or merit, or in any way deserve. Eternal life is a gift of sovereign grace. It is a gift that God gives to whomsoever he wills according to his eternal plan and purpose. He gives us eternal life, and he gives us the faith by which we lay hold of this gift of life. Our salvation is all of grace from beginning to end (Eph. 2:8).

Justification answers the question, "How can a guilty sinner be acquitted in the judgment of God and enter into eternal life?" Paul proclaims, "[A] man is justified by faith apart from observing the law" (Rom. 3:28). Martin Luther inserted the word "alone" into his translation of this verse and maintained that we are justified by faith alone, not by good works. "Justification by faith alone" has become a hallmark of evangelical theology and the touchstone of Protestant orthodoxy.

"Justification by faith alone" as a way of summarizing the biblical doctrine of justification runs into difficulty, however, when we come to the letter of James in the New Testament. James summarizes the gospel by saying that "a person is justified by what he does and not by faith alone" (Jas. 2:24). James appears to be saying exactly the opposite of what Paul is saying, and for this reason we almost uniformly tend to regard the gospel taught by James as problematic. In a letter to the editor in the September 2007 issue of *Christianity Today*, the writer confesses that he has come to question the Reformation doctrine of justification by faith alone. He says, "The case for justification by faith alone only seems to work if certain Scripture passages are excluded. For example, I've never heard preachers talk about this topic and voluntarily bring in James 2:14–26. They seem to consciously avoid James' teaching." This writer has a point. We tend to think of Paul on justification as very clear and easily understood, but we regard James as a problem to be solved rather than as a clear and authentic proclamation of saving grace.

The truth is that James is every bit as much a part of the inspired and infallible word of God as any of Paul's letters in spite of Luther's hesitancy on this point. The Holy Spirit did not give us an obscure, misleading, or defective statement of the gospel in James. What James has to say is every bit as clear, authentic, and authoritative as anything that we find in the teaching of Paul, and therefore we are taking our starting point for understanding the biblical doctrine of justification in James. From there we will go on to the teaching of Paul and our Lord in the New Testament, and then to justification under the Mosaic covenant in the Old Testament. The final chapter will take up justification under the new covenant dealing especially with matters related to our experience of this biblical truth today. In all of this I am concerned to highlight the unity and coherence of biblical teaching on this all-important doctrine of justification.

James writes in 2:24, "You see that a person is justified by what he does and not by faith alone." There are at least two questions that need to be addressed as we seek to understand the meaning of this verse. First, what does James mean by the word "justified"? What is this justification? And second, what does James mean when he says that this justification is by works and not by faith alone?

The Meaning of Justification

Verse 24 comes at the end of a line of reasoning that begins with what is really a rhetorical question in verse 14. "What good is it, my brothers, if a man claims to have faith but has no deeds? Can such faith save him?" James develops an argument in answer to this question and reaches a conclusion in verse 24. His conclusion is that a person is justified by works and not by faith alone. In verse 26 he says, "As the body without the spirit is dead, so faith without deeds is dead." The point is that "faith alone" is dead faith and therefore cannot justify.

From this line of reasoning we can see that James is using the word "justify" in a sense parallel to the word "save" in verse 14. If you are saved you are justified, and if you are justified you are saved. The same reality is in view in both verses because the affirmation in verse 24 answers the question posed in verse 14. But now we have to ask what James means by "save" in verse 14. From what are we saved? What is the salvation in view in verse 14? We get the answer to this question by reference to the preceding verses, verses 12 and 13. "Speak and act as those who are going to be judged by the law that gives freedom, because judgment without mercy will be shown to anyone who has not been merciful. Mercy triumphs over judgment!"

These verses envision a courtroom scene where human beings will stand to be judged. The criterion for judgment is "the royal law found in Scripture" (v. 8). The judge will be the lawgiver himself, the Lord God. The implication is that this law of God requires us to be merciful. If we have not shown mercy to other people we cannot expect the judge to be merciful to us. We will experience judgment without mercy, and judgment without mercy amounts to condemnation. If we have been merciful we will be acquitted in the judgment of God because "mercy triumphs over judgment!" (v. 13). Salvation in verse 14 is therefore salvation from condemnation when we stand before the Lord God to be judged. Salvation from condemnation in the judgment of God is exactly what we mean by justification. That is why James can use the word "justified" in verse 24 in answer to a question about salvation in verse 14.

At this point we can introduce two technical terms that are often used when theologians discuss the matter of justification. The justification in verse 24 can be described as *forensic*. That is, justification is a judgment declared by one who is competent to judge. Justification is a divine declaration concerning the sinner. Justification is not the moral transformation of the sinner and differs in this respect from regeneration and sanctification. Justification is not an act of regeneration or a process of sanctification. Justification is a judgment conceived and passed on the sinner by the Lord God.

The justification in verse 24 can also be described as *soteric*. The word "soteric" comes from a Greek root meaning salvation. Soteric justification has to do with the judgment that God makes concerning a sinner that leads to eternal life. It is a saving declaration that the one being judged is free from guilt and is accepted as righteous in the sight of God.

This forensic-soteric sense for justification is the one that predominates in the New Testament and especially in the writings of Paul. When James says that "a person is justified by what he does and not by faith alone," he is using the word "justify" in the same forensic-soteric sense as Paul when Paul says that "a man is justified by faith apart from observing the law" (Rom. 3:28; Gal. 2:16). It is this fact that appears to bring James into direct conflict with Paul.

We can get a clearer understanding of the justification in view in James by comparison with two passages in the gospel of Matthew. The first is Matthew 18:21–35, the Parable of the Unmerciful Servant. Our Lord tells this parable in answer to the question, "How many times shall I forgive my brother when he sins against me?" The parable tells of a servant who owed his master a large sum of money, but the master had pity on his servant and forgave him. The servant, however, demanded payment in full from one who owed him a very small amount of money. This debtor begged for mercy, but the servant threw him into prison. When the master heard what had happened, he punished his servant by reinstating his debt and consigning him to prison. Jesus makes the application by saying, "This is how my heavenly Father will treat each of you unless you forgive your brother from your heart."

The second passage is Matthew 25:31–46 where our Lord describes a judgment scene in detail. In this judgment scene, the judge who is Jesus himself separates the sheep from the goats. The sheep are persons who have shown mercy to people in need. They have fed the hungry, clothed the needy, and visited the sick. In verse 37 they are called "the righteous." The goats are those who have not shown mercy. Jesus says that the goats will go away into eternal punishment, but the sheep, the righteous ones, will enter into eternal life.

Both of these passages furnish close parallels to James 2:12, 13. In both of them we have to do with the judgment of people who have or have not shown mercy. Those who have shown mercy receive mercy, and those who have refused to show mercy are condemned. In both of these passages, as in James 2:14, the Day of Judgment is in view when Jesus will return to judge the living and the dead. Salvation in verse 14 and justification in verse 24 both mean forgiveness, deliverance from eternal punishment, and entrance into eternal life.

James is asking the question, "Can faith without deeds save a person from eternal condemnation in the Day of Judgment?" It is a rhetorical question and the implied answer is "No"; but James does not leave the matter there. He goes on to make an argument to demonstrate and prove his answer. He reaches a conclusion in verse 24 with the declaration that "A person is justified by what he does and not by faith alone." That is to say, such a person will be in the right in the judgment of God and therefore will be saved from condemnation. He will enter into eternal life. In v. 24 James uses "justify" in a forensic-soteric sense.

Because this sense seems to bring James into conflict with Paul, many students of Scripture prefer to find James using "justify" not in a forensic-soteric sense, but in a demonstrative, non-soteric sense. In the demonstrative sense "justify" takes the meaning of "show to be righteous" rather than "declare to be righteous." There are several places in the New Testament where "justify" is used, or possibly used, in this demonstrative sense. For example, Luke 10:29 and 16:15, Romans 3:3, 4, and possibly 1 Corinthians 4:4 and 1 Timothy 3:16, use justification in this demonstrative sense. If this interpretation is adopted, we are relieved of the discrepancy between James and Paul. The statement in verse 21 that Abraham was justified by what he did would not mean that he was saved (justified in the forensic-soteric sense) by what he did, but that he was shown to be a righteous man by what he did.

We can make two preliminary observations as we evaluate this demonstrative sense for "justify" in James 2. The first is that in James 2:14–26 the writer is not saying that *faith* is justified, or that *faith* is shown to be in the right, or that *faith* is shown to be genuine faith by the works that invariably accompany it. This point is true enough in itself, and it is the point James makes in verse 18 when he says "I will show you my faith by what I do." But in the three places in this passage where James uses the word "justify," they are *persons* who are said to be justified, not *faith*.

The second observation is that although "justify" can mean "show to be righteous," or "show to be just," it cannot mean, "show to be justified." When James says that Abraham and Rahab were justified by their works, he is not saying that Abraham and Rahab showed by their works that they were justified. Nor can we use this text today to argue that believers show themselves to be justified by their works. This interpretation is really a hybrid of the declarative and demonstrative senses of the word. It is a meaning that the word itself does not bear. It is not a definition offered in the standard lexicons for the Greek word that underlies "justify" and there are no examples of such a use in the Bible. The demonstrative sense is "show to be (inherently) righteous or just," not "show to have been declared just (justified forensically and savingly)."

The question now is whether James is using "justify" in the demonstrative sense. The fact that such an interpretation is possible is, of course, not proof that this interpretation is what James had in mind. The one argument in favor of this interpretation is the fact that it does provide a convenient way to reconcile Paul and James, but this is a theological argument rather than an exegetical argument.

The main problem with the demonstrative sense for "justify" is simply that it does not fit into the flow of the argument as James develops it. His point is not that a person who has faith but no works is really justified by faith alone, but simply lacks the visible evidence that he is a true believer, and cannot be shown to be a righteous person. His point is that faith without works is dead (v. 26). Such faith is useless (v. 20). It does not accomplish anything because it is dead. Such faith does not and cannot save (v. 14), and a faith that cannot save is a faith that cannot justify (v. 24).

Even if we were to adopt the sense that by works a person shows himself to be inherently righteous, it would still remain true that only the person who shows himself to be righteous in this way has a faith that saves and a faith that is not useless or dead. It would run counter to the argument of James to insist that a faith without works, a faith that cannot save, can nevertheless justify in the forensic-soteric sense. Only if "justify" in verse 24 carries the forensic-soteric sense does the verse answer the question posed in verse 14. This is the compelling argument for the forensic-soteric sense of "justify" in verse 24. James is saying that a person will stand in the judgment of God on the last day by works and not by faith alone.

The broader context in James confirms the fact that the author has in view the final judgment and a soteric justification on that day. In 5:7–9 James twice refers to the coming of the Lord and says that his coming is near. That coming would be his Second Coming at the end of the present age. When he comes he will come as a judge. Verse 9 says, "Don't grumble against each other, brothers, or you will be judged. The Judge is standing at the door!" When James says that those who grumble against each other will be judged he means that they will be condemned in the judgment. They will not be saved. The idea of a future judgment is present in other verses as well. In 3:1 James says that those of us who are teachers in the church will be judged more strictly. In 4:12 judgment and salvation are connected. "There is only one Lawgiver and Judge, the one who is able to save and destroy." Salvation and destruction are the only two possible outcomes in the final judgment. Verse 1:21 teaches us to get rid of all moral filth and to "accept the word planted in you, which can save you." Verse 5:20 tells us that if we turn a sinner from the error of his way, we will save him from death. The salvation referred to in both of these verses would have to be salvation from condemnation in the judgment of God on the last day. The last day is the day when we will all stand before the Lord God to be judged. Either we will be condemned for our sin or we will be justified and saved.

To summarize, the justification in view in James 2:24 is soteric justification. It is the salvation in view in verse 14. The passage contemplates a Day of Judgment to come when all people will appear before the Lord Jesus Christ to be judged. Will they escape from a judgment that is unto condemnation and death? James says in verse 24 that they will be justified and saved by what they do and not by faith alone. This brings us to the second question. What does James mean when he says that this forensic-soteric justification is "by works and not by faith alone?"

The Meaning of Justification by Works

The first and most important observation we must make is simply that James is not denying that justification is by faith. He is not saying that justification is by works alone. Just as faith alone is dead faith (v. 26), so also works alone are dead works (Heb. 6:1; 9:14). Rather, verses 14–26 are designed to establish justification by faith in a pointed and precise way. The one who believes in Jesus Christ as Lord and Savior will be justified and saved.

We can see how James' understanding of justification as justification by faith is established from the context of verses 14–26. James writes his letter to people who are believers. In 2:1 he calls them "my brothers," and "believers in our glorious Lord Jesus Christ." But they are believers whose faith is being tested by various trials. James says in 1:2, "Consider it pure joy, my brothers, whenever you face trials of many kinds." In the face of this testing James urges perseverance in faith. Those who are being tested must stand firm in the faith, and James offers both encouragement and assurance to that end. Those who persevere in *faith* in spite of trial and opposition "will receive the crown of life that God has promised to those who love him" (1:12). Those who are rich in *faith* will inherit the kingdom the Lord has promised to those who love him (2:5). These verses make clear that James teaches a gospel of salvation by faith in Jesus Christ. He urges faith not as a meritorious human virtue making a person worthy of being saved, but as total dependence on Jesus Christ as the only Lord and Savior.

This is the gospel he continues to declare in 2:14–26. Chapter two does not teach salvation or justification by works *apart* from faith or even justification by works in *addition* to faith. The bottom line is that justification (salvation) is by faith. Thus the justifying faith James is talking about is the same faith that Paul talks about when he says that justification is by faith and not by observing the law. Both writers have soteric faith and soteric justification in view. James and Paul cannot be set over against one another as though James taught justification by works and Paul, justification by faith. Both teach justification by faith.

But James says more about this faith when he says that justification is by works and not by faith alone (v. 24). These words focus our attention on the kind of faith that justifies and saves. Justification is by faith, but not by a faith that stands all alone devoid of action and unproductive of good works. Saving faith in Jesus Christ is a faith that works. It is a living and active faith. Only a living and active faith justifies and saves. That is the point James is making in verses 14–26.

In verse 14 James asks whether a faith that has no deeds—faith without obedience—can save. It is a rhetorical question, and the answer is "No, of course not!" This answer is illustrated in the verses that follow and is explained with examples drawn from Scripture itself.

In verses 15–17 James begins by illustrating his point using a relevant analogy. Suppose someone is without clothes and food. You wish him well but do nothing to meet the pressing need. The wish without the deed accomplishes nothing. It does not serve to clothe or to feed the needy person. In the same way, faith without deeds accomplishes nothing. It does not save and it does not justify.

This is only an illustration, but it is one that is directly relevant to the point James is making. In the earlier verses in chapter 2 James had talked about our proper attitude toward the poor. They are to be treated with the same dignity and respect with which we treat the wealthy. Verse 8 quotes the royal law, "Love your neighbor as yourself." In the language of verse 13 it is a matter of showing mercy. The illustration in verses 15–17 talks about showing mercy to persons in need, people who are cold and hungry. The wish without the deed is like faith without mercy. The illustration brings us once again into the sphere of Matthew 25:31–46. The righteous in Matthew 25 are those who show mercy to people in need. Two of the specific needs James mentions are the needs for clothing and food, the same ones that are mentioned in Matthew 25. The thought is not simply that righteous people show themselves to be truly righteous people by the help they give to those in need. Jesus is saying in Matthew 25 that only the righteous—those whose faith is wrought out in deeds—enter into eternal life.

Once again we see how closely verses 14–26 are tied in with verses 12, 13. This confirms the interpretation presented above, that James is using "justify" in a forensic-soteric sense.

Verses 18–19 make the point that true faith becomes visible in action. These verses can be compared to James 3:13. "Who is wise and understanding among you? Let him show it by his good life, by deeds done in the humility that comes from wisdom." Wisdom and understanding become visible in the good life by deeds done in humility. There is a similar argument in Matthew 11:19 (Luke 7:35). "The Son of Man came eating and drinking, and they say, 'Here is a glutton and a drunkard, a friend of tax collectors and "sinners."' But wisdom is proved right (justified; shown to be in the right) by her actions." This verse is significant because Matthew uses the word "justify," and he uses it in a demonstrative sense. Wisdom is shown to be genuine wisdom by her actions. So also you can show your faith to be genuine faith by what you do. James says that the demons also have a faith of sorts, but they show by what they do that it is not a true and saving faith. True faith will become visible in action.

Verse 14 made the point that faith without deeds has no value. It is no good. Verse 20 now asks, "[D]o you want evidence that faith without deeds is useless?" The verses that follow proceed to offer that evidence in the form of two examples drawn from the Old Testament, Abraham and Rahab. These examples are significant because of what these people represent. They stand at opposite ends of the human spectrum in three significant ways. Abraham is a Jew in covenant with the Lord, a righteous person obedient to the Lord, and a male. Rahab is a Gentile standing outside of the covenant line, a sinner as evidenced by her prostitution, and a female. Because these examples cover the extremes they also speak to everything in between. What is true for converted Jews is also true for converted Gentiles. Like Paul especially in Romans and Galatians, James is saying that there is now no difference between Jew and Gentile when it comes to justification and salvation.

Verses 21–24 present the example of Abraham. Verse 21 says that Abraham was "considered righteous" for what he did when he offered his son Isaac on the altar. Literally the verse says that Abraham was justified by works. It is striking that James uses the very form of expression that Paul rejects. For Paul, Abraham is an example of justification by faith and for James, an example of justification by works.

Verse 22 makes the point that this action of Abraham was an expression of his faith. His "faith was working with his works, and as a result of the works, faith was perfected" (New American Standard Version Update). His faith was not merely *demonstrated* by what he did, but was *completed* by what he did. Without the deed the faith would not be genuine faith. It would be useless and dead. Abraham believed God and trusted him so much that he actually proceeded to do what God told him to do. He did that in spite of the fact that he could not see how God's promise of children could be fulfilled if Isaac were to die; but Abraham trusted and obeyed. His obedience is the obedience of faith. It springs from faith and is an expression of his faith.

Verse 23 says that in this way Scripture was fulfilled. The Scripture referred to is Genesis 15:6, "Abraham believed God, and it was credited to him as righteousness." This happened at the point when the promise was given to Abraham, but of course the work of offering Isaac as a sacrifice did not happen until much later in the experience of Abraham. In the light of Genesis 15:6 it would be wrong to conclude that Abraham's faith was not credited to him as righteousness until after it had been completed by the offering of Isaac. The point is that the faith Abraham had when he believed the promise was the kind of faith that would issue in obedience. His faith in God's promise did in fact issue in obedience to the Lord when it was put to the test on Mount Moriah. The Scripture says that the faith of Abraham is completed in this act of obedience. His faith was pregnant with obedience.

What is credited or imputed to Abraham? The answer is his *faith*. The faith he had was reckoned to his account as righteousness. Faith and the obedience flowing from faith are of a piece with one another and together they constitute the righteousness of Abraham. Abraham was a righteous man. He trusted the Lord and obeyed him. This fact is recognized, acknowledged, and declared in the judgment of God. This is the man who is justified and saved, the man who believes God and who believes in God with a living, active, and obedient faith.

James makes the application to his own generation and to every generation of believers by saying in verse 24 that a person is justified by what he does, and not by faith alone. If Abraham had simply believed the promise without acting on it when his faith was tested, he would not have been justified in the judgment of God. His faith would have been dead and therefore useless. James is saying that the person who believes God, who believes in his Son, and who believes the gospel with a living, active, and obedient faith, is a righteous man. He is in the right with God now and will be saved from condemnation in the Day of Judgment. He is justified now and will be justified in the final judgment.

Verse 25 points to the example of Rahab, and the reference is to the story recorded in Joshua 2. Even though she is a prostitute (a sinner) she is considered righteous because of what she did when she gave lodging to the spies sent to Jericho by Joshua. She is justified (she is in the right) in the judgment of God because of what she did. Literally James says she was justified by works, and again the language is precisely the language that Paul rejects.

Rahab was, of course, a Gentile and therefore not included in the covenant made with Abraham and his descendants. But just as Abraham is not an example of faith without works, so also Rahab is not an example of works without faith. James makes no express mention of her faith in verse 25, but we know from the Old Testament that she was a believer and that her works were an expression of this faith. In Joshua 2:9 Rahab testifies to the spies, "I know that the Lord has given this land to you." She had heard how the Lord had delivered his people from Egypt and how Israel had destroyed the Amorite kings, Sihon and Og. This victory was from the Lord. She believed that, and she confesses her faith in verse 11, "[T]he Lord your God is God in heaven above and on the earth below."

It was because of her faith and as an expression of her faith that she offered lodging to the spies sent by Joshua. "By faith the prostitute Rahab, because she welcomed the spies, was not killed with those who were disobedient" (Heb. 11:31). She did not share in the divine judgment that fell upon those who were unbelieving and disobedient. James says that she was considered righteous for what she did. She was justified and saved by faith, by a living, active, and obedient faith, by a faith that worked.

Verses 14–26 conclude by saying that faith without works is dead. Again, these words answer the question posed in verse 14, what good is faith that has no deeds? The answer is that such faith is no good. Faith without works is dead (v. 17). It is useless (v. 20). James affirms very clearly that justification and salvation are by faith, but not by a dead faith. Justification and salvation are by a living, active, and obedient faith. This is what James means when he says that "a person is justified by what he does and not by faith alone."

In chapter 1 of his letter James pleads with his readers to demonstrate this kind of faith. He says in verse 22, "Do not merely listen to the word, and so deceive yourselves. Do what it says."

If you have faith but do not obey the word of the Lord you may think that you will be saved, but you are wrong. You are deceiving yourself. Verses 26–27 of chapter 1 make clear that true religion is not simply a matter of a bare faith in Jesus. "If anyone considers himself religious [faith alone] and yet does not keep a tight rein on his tongue, he deceives himself and his religion is worthless. Religion that God our Father accepts as pure and faultless is this: to look after orphans and widows in their distress and to keep oneself from being polluted by the world." Again, we may notice that the works James commends to us are works of mercy, works that triumph over judgment (v. 13).

We can summarize the gospel of James 2:12–26 in four points. First, James 2:24 is talking about justification in the forensic-soteric sense, not in the demonstrative sense. Second, this justification takes place on the Day of Judgment when Christ returns to judge the living and the dead. Third, those who will be justified in that day are those who believe in Jesus Christ as Lord and Savior with a living, active, and obedient faith. Fourth, faith that is not living, active, and obedient is dead faith, and dead faith will not justify and will not save.

This is the gospel according to James. Now we have the question, what is the gospel according to Paul, and how does the gospel of Paul relate to the gospel taught by James?

CHAPTER 2

Justification According to Paul

James teaches that "a person is justified by what he does and not by faith alone" (Jas. 2:24). Paul teaches that "a man is justified by faith apart from observing the law" (Rom. 3:28). In the English Standard Version the words of James are, "a person is justified by works and not by faith alone," and the words of Paul are, "one is justified by faith apart from works of the law." Therefore we have the questions, what does Paul mean, and does he contradict what James teaches? We focus our attention on Romans 3:28 because that is where the apparent difference with James shows up most sharply. As we look more closely at this verse three questions will occupy our attention. What does Paul mean by justification? What does Paul mean by faith? And finally, what are the works that Paul excludes from justification?

The Meaning of Justification

What does Paul mean by justification in Romans 3:28? We may note three things in answer to this question. First, justification is the forgiveness of sins so that we are accepted by God as righteous and receive the gift of eternal life. Second, justification is the forgiveness of sins grounded upon the imputation of the righteousness of Christ. Third, the righteousness of Christ imputed for our justification is his death and resurrection for us and in our place. In the words of Paul himself, "[Jesus] was delivered over to death for our sins and was raised to life for our justification" (Rom. 4:25). Paul makes these points clear in both the immediate context of verse 28 and the broader context of Romans.

In Romans 1 Paul spells out in detail how godlessness and wickedness come to expression in human experience. In chapter 2 he focuses more narrowly on his Jewish brothers. They have the law but they do not keep the law. They are sinners. His conclusion in 3:9 is that both Jew and Gentile stand condemned in the judgment of God. "All have sinned and fall short of the glory of God" (v. 23). Over against this condemnation of the human race Paul now sets a righteousness that comes directly from God (v. 21). This revealed righteousness is the sacrifice of atonement offered up by Jesus Christ on the cross (v. 25) and this propitiatory sacrifice demonstrates the justice of God. God had left the sins committed under the Mosaic covenant unpunished (v. 25). They were left unpunished because the blood of bulls and goats cannot really pay the penalty for sin (Heb. 10:4). The sins that were left unpunished under the old covenant have now been punished in the death of Christ, and therefore through faith in Jesus we are justified. That is to say, we obtain the forgiveness of sin.

Paul makes clear that justification is the forgiveness of sin grounded in the righteousness of Jesus Christ. That righteousness is his propitiatory sacrifice offered on the cross in obedience to the will of his Father in heaven. When Paul says in verse 28 that a man is justified by faith, he means that his sins are forgiven by faith. This faith is faith in the blood of Jesus (v. 25), and the blood of Jesus atones for sin.

This conclusion from the immediate context of 3:28 is confirmed in the broader context of Romans. First, in 4:6 Paul describes justification as the imputation of righteousness apart from works of the law. "David says the same thing when he speaks of the blessedness of the man to whom God credits righteousness apart from works." Then he quotes Psalm 32:1, 2, "Blessed are they whose transgressions are forgiven, whose sins are covered. Blessed is the man whose sin the Lord will never count against him." Here Paul virtually defines justification as the forgiveness of sin. He implies that when we read about the forgiveness of sin in the Old Testament we are reading about justification. When Paul says in verse 4 that God justifies the wicked, he means that God forgives the sin of the wicked because of the cross of Christ.

Second, in 4:25 Paul writes, "[Jesus] was delivered over to death for our sins and was raised to life for our justification." By his death Jesus paid the penalty for sin. His resurrection on the third day certifies that the penalty for sin has been paid in full and that therefore the justice of God has been satisfied. The death and resurrection of Jesus secure our justification, and that is to say, they secure the forgiveness of our sin.

Third, Paul writes in 5:8–9, "But God demonstrates his own love for us in this: While we were still sinners, Christ died for us. Since we have now been justified by his blood, how much more shall we be saved from God's wrath through him!" We are sinners, and Christ died to deal with the guilt of sin. Specifically the *blood* of Christ justifies us. This justification can be nothing other than the forgiveness of the sin that would otherwise serve to condemn us. The blood of Jesus justifies us because it pays the penalty for sin.

Fourth, Paul writes in 5:18, "Consequently, just as the result of one trespass was condemnation for all men, so also the result of one act of righteousness was justification that brings life for all men." The one trespass is the sin of Adam in eating the forbidden fruit. Corresponding to this is the "one act of righteousness." This one act of righteousness is the righteousness from God that Paul wrote about earlier in Romans 3:22. It is the sacrifice of atonement (v. 25), the death of Jesus on the cross. This one act obtains our justification, the forgiveness of our sin. In verse 19 Paul writes, "For just as through the disobedience of the one man the many were made sinners, so also through the obedience of the one man the many will be made righteous." The disobedience that makes us sinners is the one trespass of Adam spoken of in the preceding verse. So also the obedience that makes us righteous is the one act of righteousness also spoken of in the preceding verse. We are constituted righteous by God when he justifies us by forgiving our sin.

Fifth, we may also appeal to Paul's sermon preached in Pisidian Antioch as recorded in Acts 13. In this sermon Paul gives extensive attention to the death of Christ and his subsequent resurrection as foretold in the Old Testament. The death and resurrection of Christ are the ground of our salvation. He concludes in verses 38–39, "Therefore, my brothers, I want you to know that through Jesus the *forgiveness of sins* is proclaimed to you. Through him everyone who believes is *justified* from everything you could not be justified from by the Law of Moses" (italics added). In these words Paul equates justification with the forgiveness of sins. The Law of Moses did not justify because as Paul has said, God left sins committed under the old covenant unpunished (Rom. 3:25). Strictly speaking there was no forgiveness in the Mosaic covenant because the blood of bulls and goats cannot atone for sin. Forgiveness was possible under the old covenant only because the sacrificial system put true believers ultimately under the blood of Jesus. It is really the blood of Jesus that justifies us. That is to say, our sins are forgiven in his blood.

To summarize, what is justification in Romans 3:28? Justification is the forgiveness of sin so that we are accepted by God as righteous and receive the gift of eternal life. The ground of justification—the basis on which forgiveness is granted—is the suffering and death of our Lord. This is the one act of righteousness imputed to us for our justification. Jesus' resurrection on the third day testifies to the efficacy of this atoning sacrifice. "He was delivered over to death for our sins and was raised to life for our justification" (Rom. 4:25).

The Meaning of Faith

Paul makes clear in Romans 3:28 that justification comes by faith, and so we have the second question, what is the meaning of faith in Romans 3:28? What is the faith that justifies sinners?

First of all, justifying faith is faith in Jesus; but Paul can also speak of justifying faith simply as faith in God. In Romans 4:3 Paul quotes Genesis 15:6 and says, "Abraham believed God." This faith in God is justifying faith. Abraham believed God; he believed the promises God made to him. Romans 4:5 describes new covenant faith also as faith in God. "However, to the man who does not work but trusts God who justifies the wicked, his faith is credited as righteousness." The faith of Abraham is commended to us as exemplary. We must walk in the footsteps of the faith that our father Abraham had (v. 12). Justifying faith under the new covenant cannot be less than faith in God, faith in his word, and faith in the promise of redemption.

But now that our righteousness is embodied in the person and work of Jesus Christ, the incarnate God, justifying faith is more specifically faith in Jesus. "This righteousness from God comes through faith in Jesus Christ to all who believe" (Rom. 3:22). God "justifies those who have faith in Jesus" (v. 26). Faith in Jesus means trusting Jesus, accepting, receiving, and resting upon Jesus for the pardon of sin and the title to everlasting life. Paul is even more specific. Justifying faith is faith in the *blood* of Jesus (v. 25). The blood of Jesus atones for sin and is the ground of our forgiveness. Romans 5:9 says explicitly that we are justified (forgiven) by faith in the blood of Jesus. Because justification is the pardon of sins, justifying faith could not be other than faith in Jesus and specifically faith in his shed blood. The shed blood of Jesus atones for sin and is the ground of our pardon.

Second, justifying faith is a penitent faith. In Romans 2 Paul indicts his Jewish brethren because they commit the very sins which they condemn in others. God's judgment has not yet fallen on them because God is kind and patient. He is longsuffering. The kindness and patience of God are designed to lead sinners to repentance (v. 4). The impenitent are storing up the wrath of God for the Day of Judgment; but the penitent, those who turn away from sin and persevere in doing good, will enter into eternal life (v. 7). On this background it is inconceivable that justifying faith can be anything but a penitent faith.

Paul says in Romans 4:5 that God justifies the wicked. This does not mean that God justifies all those who qualify as wicked whether or not they believe. Nor does it mean that God justifies the wicked who remain impenitent and persevere in their wickedness. God justifies the wicked who repent, who turn away from sin with deep sorrow and who turn to Jesus for pardon. They will be forgiven in the judgment of God. The believer who repents of his sin will be justified.

This conclusion is fully in line with the character of Paul's evangelistic message as described in the Book of Acts. In Athens Paul proclaims, "In the past God overlooked such ignorance, but now he commands all people everywhere to repent. For he has set a day when he will judge the world with justice by the man he has appointed" (Acts 17:30–31). Reference to the Day of Judgment brings us immediately into the sphere of justification. Paul is saying that if we do not repent of sin we will not be justified in the judgment of God.

When Paul preached the gospel he demanded both faith and repentance. "I have declared to both Jews and Greeks that they must turn to God in repentance and have faith in our Lord Jesus" (Acts 20:21). In this verse repentance is even named before faith. Saving faith must be a penitent faith because one day God will judge the world by his Son. If we expect to be justified in that judgment we must repent of sin. Further, repentance is more than a change of heart and mind. It is a change of will and deed. Paul declares, "First to those in Damascus, then to those in Jerusalem and in all Judea, and to the Gentiles also, I preached that they should repent and turn to God and prove their repentance by their deeds" (Acts 26:20).

Third, justifying faith is not only a penitent faith but also an obedient faith. As faith and repentance are inseparably intertwined, so also repentance and obedience are inseparably intertwined. Justifying and saving faith is a penitent and obedient faith.

In Romans 1:5 Paul describes the task assigned to him as an apostle. He is commissioned "to call people from among all the Gentiles to the obedience that comes from faith." In Romans 15:18 he declares that he glories in nothing but what Christ has accomplished through him "in leading the Gentiles to obey God." What Paul says here is consistent with the way he describes his ministry in Acts. The obedience he calls for is not faith alone, but faith that entails the obedience to God's word that flows out of faith and repentance.

Paul calls not only Gentiles, but also Jews to this same faith-obedience to Christ. In Romans 2 Paul speaks of the necessity of repentance that becomes evident in doing good. He says God will give eternal life "to those who by persistence in doing good seek glory, honor and immortality" (v. 7). This kind of obedience is the expression of a saving faith in God and in his Son. Paul pleads with both Jew and Gentile "to walk in the footsteps of the faith that our father Abraham had before he was circumcised" (Rom. 4:12). The faith of Abraham was an obedient faith, a faith that moved him to leave Ur of the Chaldees when he did not know where he was going (Heb. 11:8). It was a faith that moved him to offer up Isaac at the command of God when he could not see how the promise of God could be fulfilled except through Isaac.

In Galatians 5:6 Paul writes, "For in Christ Jesus neither circumcision nor uncircumcision has any value. The only thing that counts is faith expressing itself through love." Faith that expresses itself through love is an obedient faith, and this obedient faith is justifying faith. In verse 4 Paul mentions justification explicitly. In verse 5 he says, "By faith we eagerly await through the Spirit the righteousness for which we hope." In verse 6 we are clearly in the sphere of judgment and justification. Justifying faith is obedient faith.

In Galatians 5:13 Paul says that we are free from the law. That is, we do not now serve God under the old, Mosaic covenant that prevailed from Sinai to the advent of Christ. But this fact is not a license for immorality as though there were no law at all. We are called to serve one another in love, and love is the fulfillment of what the law of the old covenant is all about. Believers are free from the law, that is, free from the Mosaic system as a way of life; but according to Romans 8:3 they are not free from the righteous requirements of the law.

In Galatians 5:6 Paul sets faith over against circumcision and uncircumcision. "Circumcision and uncircumcision" refers to the presence or absence of works of the Mosaic law. In Galatians 6:15, he contrasts the new creation with circumcision and uncircumcision. In 1 Corinthians 7:19 he contrasts keeping God's commandments with circumcision and uncircumcision. "Circumcision is nothing and uncircumcision is nothing. Keeping God's commands is what counts." Therefore when Paul speaks of faith expressing itself through love, he is talking about keeping God's commandments. He is talking about a new creation. Faith, repentance, and obedience are possible in the experience of sinners only by grace, because we are a new creation. Paul writes in Ephesians 2:10, "For we are God's workmanship, created in Christ Jesus to do good works, which God prepared in advance for us to do." Similarly he writes in Ephesians 4:24 that we are "created to be like God in true righteousness and holiness."

This living, active, and obedient faith is clearly differentiated from works of the law. In the language of Romans 2, those who are seeking to be justified and saved by the works of the law do not keep the law. They only hear the law but do not do what it says. In contrast to that, Paul describes true believers as those who repent of sin and who seek to do what is good according to God's law. They are recreated in Christ for this very purpose, and they will inherit eternal life. This is what Paul declares in Romans 2:13, "For it is not those who hear the law who are righteous in God's sight, but it is those who obey the law who will be declared righteous." Their obedience is the obedience of faith, that is, the expression of faith or the fruit of faith. Those who believe in Jesus with this kind of faith will be justified. Paul says in verse 16, "This [justification of those who obey the law] will take place on the day when God will judge men's secrets through Jesus Christ, as my gospel declares." Romans 2:13 is really the Pauline equivalent of James 2:24.

The believer, who believes in Jesus Christ with a living, active, penitent, and obedient faith, is the righteous man who lives by faith (Rom. 1:17). He is not without sin, sin that would otherwise condemn him; but his sin is forgiven in the blood of Jesus. The righteous who live by faith are those whom God has recreated in his image in righteousness and holiness. They look to Jesus for the forgiveness of their sins, and they walk with the Lord day by day in repentance and obedience. This is the kind of faith that is imputed to Abraham for righteousness. This is the faith by which we are justified today according to Romans 3:28. This is what Paul is talking about when he says in Romans 1:17, "The righteous will live by faith."

Now it becomes necessary to understand how this faith and this righteousness have nothing to do with justification by works of the law.

The Works Excluded from Justification

In Romans 3:28 Paul says that we are justified by faith "apart from observing the law." Literally he says we are justified by faith "without the works of the law." What are these "works of the law" that are excluded from justification? There are at least three things we should note in answer to this question.

First, by "works of the law" Paul refers to the Mosaic covenant as such. This is the arrangement under which God's people (Israel) served the Lord from Mt. Sinai to the advent of Christ. These works of the law are not simply the ceremonial laws of the Mosaic covenant, but the whole Mosaic system as a way of life, the old covenant. With the death and resurrection of Christ we now serve the Lord under the new covenant. Paul is saying in Romans 3:28 that we are not justified by clinging to the Mosaic covenant as though it were still operative. This can be clearly seen from the very next verse, verse 29.

In verse 29 Paul asks, "Or is God the God of Jews only? Is he not the God of Gentiles too?" His answer is, "Yes, of Gentiles too." The all-important word "or" at the beginning of verse 29 is found in the Greek text, but the New International Version wrongly omits this word from its translation. Other modern translations, however, do include it. The point Paul is making is that if justification comes by the works of the law even after the advent of Christ, then Gentiles cannot be justified or saved. The reason is not that the Gentiles cannot *keep* the law, but that they do not *have* the law. They do not have the law because the Mosaic covenant was made with Israel and with no other nation. In Romans 2:15 Paul says that the Gentiles show the requirements of the law written on their hearts. Paul does not say that the law itself is written on their hearts, but that the requirements of the law are written on their hearts. The Gentiles are not embraced within the Mosaic covenant. The law given from Mt. Sinai was given only to Israel (Ps. 147:19–20). If now, under the new covenant, justification comes by the works of the law, then Gentiles would continue to be excluded from God's saving purpose. That is Paul's argument in verse 29.

The gospel Paul preached was a gospel for both Jew and

Gentile. This is a major emphasis in both Romans and Galatians. It was a most difficult point for most Jews to grasp—the idea that God's saving purpose now included Gentiles as well as Jews. Paul's insistence on this point is the reason for much of the Jewish opposition to his gospel. Paul says there is only one God, and he is the God of both Jew and Gentile. But he cannot be that if justification comes by works of the law. Then he is the God of the Jews only. But through faith in Jesus both Jew and Gentile are justified. As Paul says in Galatians 2:14, neither Jew nor Gentile will be justified by following "Jewish customs." You will not be justified by living according to Jewish religious regulations as prescribed in the old Mosaic covenant as though that covenant were still in force. When you do that you separate yourself from Christ (Gal. 5:4), and apart from Christ there is neither justification nor life!

Second, by works of the law Paul means obedience to a limited selection of laws found in the Law of Moses and in tradition. In Romans 1, 2, and 3 Paul is concerned to demonstrate that both Gentile and Jew are under the wrath of God because of sin. In particular, the Jews have the law of God because it was given to them on Mt. Sinai, but they disobey this law. In 2:17–24 Paul demonstrates that their disobedience is no small matter touching on some minor points that require a lot of personal microscopic self-examination to uncover. He says that because of what the vast majority of his fellow-countrymen are doing, "God's name is blasphemed among the Gentiles." Such impenitent lawbreakers are covenant breakers, and they cannot be justified or saved (Rom. 2:12, 13, 16).

These people, however, do not see themselves as sinners in need of repentance and forgiveness. The reason for this is that they do "works of the law." Paul presents his former self as an example of this sort of mentality. In Philippians 3:4–6 he writes, "If anyone else thinks he has reasons to put confidence in the flesh, I have more: circumcised on the eighth day, of the people of Israel, of the tribe of Benjamin, a Hebrew of Hebrews; in regard to the law, a Pharisee; as for zeal, persecuting the church; as for legalistic righteousness, faultless." Paul thought of himself as justified because of his heritage, training, and pursuit of legalistic righteousness. He thought of himself as acceptable to God just as he was and therefore entitled to eternal life. He thought of himself as faultless! That he was in fact a condemned sinner under the wrath of God is evident from his confession that he persecuted the church.

Paul says the mere fact that a Jew is circumcised (a work of the law) means nothing if he breaks the law in other respects (Rom. 2:25). The kind of people Paul is thinking about are condemned by our Lord in Matthew 23. Yes, they give to the Lord a tenth of their spices—mint, dill, and cumin. These are works of the law that they do; but they neglect the more important matters of the law—justice, mercy, and faithfulness (Matt. 23:23).

The problem has a long history in Israel as evidenced by Isaiah 64:6. Isaiah says, "All of us have become like one who is unclean, and all our righteous acts are like filthy rags." By "righteous acts" Isaiah does not mean good works, that is to say, works done in faith, according to the law of God, and for the glory of God. He means "works of the law," selective acts of obedience that are designed to cover up the massive disobedience of which the people were guilty. Isaiah describes such works of the law, for example, in chapter 1, verses 10–17. These works of the law are, indeed, no better than filthy rags. People who are seeking to be justified by such works of the law are sinners who do not confess their sin but pretend to be righteous. Paul says that they stand condemned by the very law in which they think they find their righteousness.

Third, works of the law are works that are done without faith. The law does, indeed, condemn our sin, and by the law we become conscious of our sin if we really hear what it says (Rom. 3:20). What the law demands is confession of sin and repentance, and what the law promises is forgiveness through the shedding of blood. It offers justification and salvation by faith in God; but those seeking to be justified by works of the law have rejected the way of faith, and that means they have actually rejected the law. A law that they have really rejected could not possibly justify them. Jesus says to such people, "Your accuser is Moses, on whom your hopes are set. If you believed Moses, you would believe me, for he wrote about me" (John 5:45–46). These people really did not believe Moses! They are not justified because justification is by faith and these people are unbelievers! Those seeking to be justified by the works of the law were rejecting the biblical method of justification by faith.

Over against this Paul presents Abraham in chapter 4 as the great example of justification by faith. Abraham trusted God and acted accordingly. His was an obedient faith. He was not without sin; but his sins were forgiven, and he walked with the Lord as a faithful covenant keeper. Every Jew as well as every Gentile who wants to be right with God must "walk in the footsteps of the faith that our father Abraham had before he was circumcised" (Rom. 4:12). Faith was always the method of justification. That is why Paul can summarize the doctrine of the new covenant with a quotation from the old covenant. "The righteous will live by his faith" (Hab. 2:4).

Those who were seeking to be justified by works of the law had rejected the way of faith.

Paul makes this point explicitly in Romans 9:30–32. "What then shall we say? That the Gentiles, who did not pursue righteousness, have obtained it, a righteousness that is by faith; but Israel, who pursued a law of righteousness, has not attained it. Why not? Because they pursued it not by faith but as if it were by works." These works of the law were not good works. They were not the obedience of faith wrought by the power of God. They were works done in the strength of human flesh in order to obtain the justifying verdict of God.

"Works of the law" look for and expect a reward that is an earned wage rather than a freely bestowed gift. They do not represent a righteousness from God, but a righteousness produced by the sinner. "Since they did not know the righteousness that comes from God and sought to establish their own, they did not submit to God's righteousness" (Rom. 10:3). These were people who were confident in their own righteousness. In his own case Paul calls it a righteousness of his own making that comes from the law (Phil. 3:9). It is confidence in the flesh (vs. 3, 4).

With this stance they had in effect transformed the Law of Moses from a revelation of God's gracious saving purpose in the world into a program of salvation earned by the merit of works. The works of the law are the works of meritorious self-righteousness that only serve to mask gross sin and disobedience. By the grace of God Paul comes to the point where he throws them all away as so much rubbish in order that he might gain Christ and his righteousness (Phil. 3:8), the righteousness that comes down from heaven (Rom. 3:21, 22).

Because these people did not believe Moses they did not understand the way of salvation by grace through faith. Therefore when Jesus came proclaiming the way of salvation through faith in himself as the Son of God, they rejected Jesus. They did not see themselves as sinners who needed to confess sin or to repent of it. Like the Pharisee in the parable they trusted in their own righteousness (Luke 18:9–14). Paul says in Galatians 5:4, "You who are trying to be justified by law have been alienated from Christ; you have fallen away from grace." If we are alienated from Christ we lose all hope of justification and salvation from the wrath to come.

There is a vast difference between the works of the law that Paul everywhere condemns and the obedience of faith that Paul everywhere commends and encourages. In the language of Micah 6:7, 8, it is the difference between ten thousand of rivers of oil— works of the law and much more! —and doing justice, loving mercy, and walking humbly with your God. Therefore Paul does not come into conflict with himself when he declares that justification comes by a penitent and obedient faith, and not by works of the law. By the same token Paul does not come into conflict with James when he says that justification comes by faith without the works of the law. Both apostles are saying that we are justified by faith in Jesus, and that this faith is a living faith. It is a penitent and obedient faith.

The gospel that James and Paul proclaimed is, of course, not a gospel that they created out of thin air. It is the gospel that they received from Jesus and is the gospel that Jesus himself taught. We turn now to the gospels to see how this is so.

CHAPTER 3

Justification According to Our Lord

W hen we want to know about the biblical doctrine of justifi- cation we usually turn first to the letters of Paul and specifi- cally to Romans and Galatians because it is in these letters that we find the word "justification" used most frequently. But the teaching of Paul rests squarely on the gospel as taught by our Lord, and we find the gospel our Lord taught in the gospels of Matthew, Mark, Luke, and John. That is where we need to go now to find out what our Lord taught about the justification of a sinner before God.

To appreciate this point we need to remember what we have already discovered from our study of Paul and James. Justification is the forgiveness of sin, and the faith that justifies is a living, ac- tive, penitent, and obedient faith. Jesus preached the forgiveness of sin and he called sinners to repentance so that their sins might be forgiven. Further, he taught these penitent sinners who became his disciples to obey his commands. These are the three points we need to appreciate as we survey the teaching of Jesus on justifica- tion. First, Jesus preached the forgiveness of sins. Second, Jesus called sinners to repentance. And third, Jesus taught penitent sin- ners to obey his commands.

Jesus Preached the Forgiveness of Sin

The idea that God forgives sin was, of course, nothing new for the Jews to whom Jesus ministered in the days of his flesh. The sacrificial system given to Moses on Mt. Sinai was designed to re- veal this great truth to Israel. The way the Lord communicated the grace of justification under the old covenant was through the sacrifice of bulls and goats. The revelation of the sacrificial system demonstrates that the Mosaic covenant is gracious through and through. It reveals God's readiness and willingness to forgive sin in spite of the fact that human beings do not deserve to be forgiven. Building on the Old Testament, Jesus taught that our Father in heaven forgives sin. He said, for example, "if you forgive men when they sin against you, your heavenly Father will also forgive you" (Matt. 6:14). Jesus' teaching that the Father forgives sin would startle no one. Of course our Father in heaven forgives sin! What is new in Jesus' teaching—and what is startlingly new—is the fact that Jesus himself claims to forgive sin!

This new reality was anticipated in the prophecy of Zechariah when the infant John the Baptist was presented in the temple. John would prepare for the Messiah by giving the people the knowledge of salvation through the forgiveness of their sins (Luke 1:77). Zechariah speaks as though something entirely new was at hand, as though Israel had never known the way of salvation or the forgiveness of sins. In a very real sense this was true. Paul writes in Romans 3:25 that God had left the sins committed beforehand (under the old covenant) unpunished. That was so because the blood of bulls and goats could not really take away the guilt and corruption of sin. But now the day has come when God would really forgive sin, and he would do that through the redemptive work of his Son, the Lord Jesus Christ.

Toward the beginning of his public ministry Jesus performed the miracle of healing a paralytic. The miracle is recorded in all three of the synoptic gospels (Matt. 9:1–8; Mark 2:1–12; Luke 5:17–26). Some men brought a paralyzed man to Jesus in a rather creative way with the hope and expectation that Jesus would heal him. Jesus responded to their actions by saying to the paralytic, "Son, your sins are forgiven." These words riled Jewish authorities, and they accused him of blasphemy because he claimed to forgive sin. They maintained, and rightly so, that only God can forgive sin. What they did not see or accept was the fact that Jesus was God. He was Immanuel, God with us, God with the power to forgive sin. This is the point of the story and of the miraculous healing. Jesus healed this man so "that you may know that the Son of Man has authority on earth to forgive sins."

On another occasion a woman who had led a sinful life came

to Jesus while he was eating in the home of a Pharisee (Luke 7:36–50). She wet the feet of Jesus with her tears and wiped them with her hair. Then she poured perfume on his feet and kissed them. Jesus said to the woman, "Your sins are forgiven." This saying caused consternation among the guests. They said among themselves, "Who is this who even forgives sins?" Jesus exposed the self-righteousness of his host, but he also revealed himself once again as the Son of God with power to forgive sin.

This is the gospel that we find in the gospels. Jesus is the Son of God and he has come to earth to forgive sin. No doubt Jesus preached this message of forgiveness throughout his public ministry. Even to his dying moment he proclaims forgiveness as he pleads with his Father to forgive those who are putting him to death. "Father, forgive them, for they do not know what they are doing" (Luke 23:34).

Of course it is the cross itself that explains why God the Father can forgive sin and why Jesus can forgive sin. The wages of sin is death, and in his death Jesus died in the place of his people to pay the wages of sin so that they might be forgiven. "Without the shedding of blood there is no forgiveness" (Heb. 9:22). That is the great lesson of the Old Testament. Jesus shed his blood so that we might be forgiven, so that we might be justified. As Paul says in Romans 5:9, we are justified through faith in the blood of Jesus.

When Jesus instituted the sacrament of the Lord's Supper he took the cup, gave thanks, and offered it to his disciples. He said to them, "This is my blood of the covenant, which is poured out for many for the forgiveness of sins" (Matt. 26:28). Some Greek manuscripts have the reading, "This is my blood of the *new* covenant," and so it is. The blood of the new covenant is poured out for the forgiveness of sins. Because of the blood of Jesus the prophecy of Jeremiah 31:31–34 is fulfilled and the new covenant is established. "I will be their God and they will be my people. . . . I will forgive their wickedness and remember their sins no more" (Heb. 8:10, 12).

We cannot leave this point without referring to the parable of the Pharisee and the Tax Collector (Luke 18:9–14). This is one of two places in the gospels where the word "justify" is used in the Pauline forensic-soteric sense. (The other place is Matthew 12:37.) The Pharisee prayed thanking God that he was not evil like other men and he pointed out the good works he had done for God. Here was a man who was just or righteous in his own estimation. He thought that he had no sin to confess, that he did not need to repent, and that he did not need to be forgiven. The Tax Collector, on the other hand, prayed, "God, have mercy on me, a sinner." Here was a sinner who acknowledged and confessed his sin before the Lord asking only for mercy. Jesus said, "I tell you that this man, rather than the other, went home justified before God." The Lord forgave his sin. This is what we mean by justification. The sinner is forgiven and is therefore now acceptable before God. He is in a right relationship with the Lord God. He is justified.

The grace of justification is not a Pauline peculiarity, and Paul has no monopoly on the doctrine. Jesus proclaims justification throughout his public ministry because he proclaims the forgiveness of sin. Therefore when we want to know about justification we can just as well turn to the gospels as to Romans and Galatians. Paul builds his ministry on what he has learned from our Lord.

Jesus Called Sinners to Repentance

Jesus began his public ministry by calling sinners to repentance. "From that time on Jesus began to preach, 'Repent, for the kingdom of heaven is near'" (Matt. 4:17). This is the same message that John the Baptist had been preaching. Therefore we can better understand the ministry of Jesus by taking a closer look at the ministry of John.

What is the repentance that John demands from those who heard him? The word itself indicates a change of mind and heart. John asked the covenant people of God to acknowledge and confess their sins (Matt. 3:6). But more than that, he told them to turn away from sin, to do what was right, and to "produce fruit in keeping with repentance" (Matt. 3:8; Luke 3:8). John spells out in detail what this entails.

"What should we do then?" the crowd asked. John answered, "The man with two tunics should share with him who has none, and the one who has food should do the same." Tax collectors also came to be baptized. "Teacher," they asked, "what should we do?" "Don't collect any more than you are required to," he told them. Then some soldiers asked him, "And what should we do?" He replied, "Don't extort money and don't accuse people falsely—be content with your pay" (Luke 3:10–14).

This list is by no means comprehensive or exhaustive, but gives a sampling of what is involved in true repentance.

This demand for repentance is also, of course, a demand for faith. In asking people to believe his message John is preparing the way for Messiah and is really asking people to believe in Jesus. Paul testifies in Acts 19:4, "John's baptism was a baptism of repentance. He told the people to believe in the one coming after him, that is, in Jesus." Repentance and faith are inseparably intertwined in his ministry. What John is calling for in his preaching is a penitent and obedient faith.

Of special significance for the doctrine of justification is the fact that John preaches repentance, which is unto the forgiveness of sin. "And so John came, baptizing in the desert region and preaching a baptism of repentance for the forgiveness of sins" (Mark 1:4; Luke 3:3). This is the good news that John is privileged to proclaim, the news that sinners who repent of their sin will be forgiven. The point here is that repentance is necessary for the forgiveness of sin. Those who believed the message of John, who submitted to his baptism and turned away from sin, were forgiven. The baptism that John administered was a sign and seal of the transformation that had taken place in their lives. Those who do not repent will not experience the forgiveness of sin.

Further, there is urgency in John's message of repentance because of the imminence of judgment. Jesus is coming to judge and those who remain impenitent will fall under his judgment. Their sins will not be forgiven. "The ax is already at the root of the trees, and every tree that does not produce good fruit will be cut down and thrown into the fire" (Matt. 3:10). Jesus will come. "His winnowing fork is in his hand, and he will clear his threshing floor, gathering his wheat into the barn and burning up the chaff with unquenchable fire" (Matt. 3:12). The wheat represents those who are believing and penitent. The chaff are those who are unbelieving and impenitent.

The fact that John preaches the forgiveness of sin and warns of a judgment to come brings us into the sphere of justification. Justification is a forensic concept, having to do with a judgment that is made and declared. Further, the judgment John announces is the ultimate judgment with the Son of God sitting as judge. It will issue either in eternal life or in eternal death. Thus the justification in view is both forensic and soteric as it is in Paul and in James.

As we have noted, Jesus began his ministry with the same message John preached, "Repent, for the kingdom of heaven is near." This emphasis on repentance continued throughout his ministry. Jesus testifies that he has come to call sinners to repentance (Luke 5:31). The parables of the Lost Sheep, the Lost Coin, and the Lost Son in Luke 15 all have repentance as their theme. Jesus testifies to the joy in heaven over the sinner who repents. This joy in heaven contrasts with the deep sorrow that Jesus feels because God's own people do not come to repentance. In spite of the miraculous demonstration of divine grace in their midst, cities like Korazin, Bethsaida, and Capernaum do not repent. Jesus says that these cities will come under divine judgment because of their obstinacy and their impenitence (Matt. 11:20–24).

Because Jesus continues and expands the prophetic ministry of John, the repentance he demands is the same repentance that John demanded. It is not only a sorrow for sin, but also a turning away from sin in order to pursue righteousness according to the word of God. This point is made especially clear in a passage like Mark 9:43–48.

> If your hand causes you to sin, cut it off. It is better for you
> to enter life maimed than with two hands to go into hell,
> where the fire never goes out. And if your foot causes you to

sin, cut it off. It is better for you to enter life crippled than to have two feet and be thrown into hell. And if your eye causes you to sin, pluck it out. It is better for you to enter the kingdom of God with one eye than to have two eyes and be thrown into hell, where "the worm does not die, and the fire is not quenched."

Jesus is saying that those who willfully persist in sin will not be saved.

In Luke 13:1–5 Jesus makes clear that the only alternatives are repentance or destruction. He reminds his listeners of the Galileans who were put to death by Pilate, and the eighteen persons on whom the Tower of Siloam fell. Jesus says, "Unless you repent, you too will all perish." If sinners are going to survive the judgment they must repent. They must turn away from sin and begin to pursue righteousness. In Matthew 23 Jesus pronounces seven woes upon teachers of the law who pretend to be righteous because they do works of the law, but in reality they are sinners who break the law and who remain impenitent. They are not justified or saved by their works of the law.

Jesus not only preached repentance himself, but also commanded his disciples to proclaim the same message. Jesus sent the Twelve out two by two and told them to preach the nearness of the kingdom and the necessity of repentance (Luke 10:11, 13, 14). Just prior to his ascension Jesus appeared to his disciples and said to them, "This is what is written: The Christ will suffer and rise from the dead on the third day, and repentance and forgiveness of sins will be preached in his name to all nations, beginning at Jerusalem" (Luke 24:46, 47). The New International Version translates these verses as "repentance *and* forgiveness will be preached." The underlying Greek original says, "repentance *for* forgiveness of sins"; and it is so translated in the New American Standard Version.

In Matthew the Great Commission takes this form: "Therefore go and make disciples of all nations, baptizing them in the name of the Father and of the Son and of the Holy Spirit, and teaching them to obey everything I have commanded you. And surely I am with you always, to the very end of the age" (Matt. 28:19, 20). The baptism of John was a baptism of repentance for the remission of sin. The baptism called for in the Great Commission is also a baptism of repentance for the remission of sin as is evident from the way Peter preached on the Day of Pentecost as he carried out the Great Commission. When the people heard him and were "cut to the heart" in sorrow for sin, they asked, "What shall we do?" Peter answered, "Repent and be baptized, every one of you, in the name of Jesus Christ for the forgiveness of your sins. And you will receive the gift of the Holy Spirit" (Acts 2:38). Jesus commanded his disciples to preach repentance and that is what they did.

It is essential to note that the gospels do not present repentance simply as the inevitable fruit, or consequence, or result of faith and justification. The gospels do not present repentance as coming after justification, or after the forgiveness of sins, as evidence of a prior justification. Repentance is presented as *unto* the forgiveness of sin and as *unto* justification. Sinners must repent in order to be forgiven. They must repent in order to be justified and saved. Therefore we have to say that in the teaching of our Lord repentance is necessary for justification. There is no forgiveness of sin and therefore no justification without repentance.

Jesus Taught Penitent Sinners to Obey His Commands

True repentance will come to expression in obedience to the will of God. This is inevitable because repentance is not only a hatred of sin but also a turning from sin and a turning to righteousness. The truly penitent sinner cannot return to the lifestyle from which he has turned away. John came calling sinners to repentance, but as Jesus also says in Matthew 21:32, "John came to you to show you the way of righteousness." John preached both repentance and obedience. The change of heart called for in repentance makes itself evident in new patterns of obedience to the Lord God. The demand for repentance is of a piece with the demand for obedience to the Lord.

In the ministry of our Lord we see that the call for repentance is coupled with teaching penitent sinners to obey his commands. We see that very early in his ministry when he went up on a mountainside and his disciples came to him. Jesus began to teach them in what we call the Sermon on the Mount. Jesus presents detailed instruction concerning the righteousness of the kingdom he is building. In this sermon our Lord teaches his followers the sanctity of life, the sanctity of marriage, and the sanctity of a promise. He teaches principles of love and compassion for our neighbors, love and dependence upon the Lord in our daily lives, and much more. The Sermon on the Mount spells out what faith in Jesus Christ means and what becoming a disciple of Christ entails.

The Sermon begins with a series of beatitudes in which the Lord spells out the blessings that will attend righteousness in his kingdom. These blessings include seeing God, being identified as sons of God, inheriting the earth, and receiving the kingdom of heaven. In language that reminds us of James 2:12, 13, Jesus says that God will show mercy to those who are merciful. It is a short step from these sayings to recognizing that issues of eternal weal and woe are suspended on the response of obedience. In Matthew 5:20 Jesus says, "For I tell you that unless your righteousness surpasses that of the Pharisees and the teachers of the law, you will certainly not enter the kingdom of heaven." In this verse Jesus is not talking about the imputation of his own perfect active obedience to sinners as the ground of their justification, but about the righteous behavior he is describing in the Sermon.

The righteousness of the Pharisees is "works of the law." These are the kinds of works that both Jesus and Paul roundly condemn because they left the weightier matters of the law, justice and mercy, undone (Matt. 23:23). Their works were not the works of faith. Jesus is saying to his followers, "You must not be satisfied with that kind of righteousness. You must press on to be the disciples I am calling you to be, disciples who do justly, love mercy, and walk humbly with your God" (Mic. 6:8). That is the kind of faith in Jesus that gives entrance to the kingdom of heaven.

In the parables of our Lord we also see the kind of faith to which he was calling his disciples. Matthew 13:1–23 records the Parable of the Sower in which seed falls on four different kinds of ground. The seed represents the word of God and the four different kinds of ground represent the different ways in which God's word is received. There is faith that lacks understanding, faith that does not bear up under trial, and faith that is choked to death by other cares and interests. The faith that Jesus proclaims and commends is a faith that understands and that endures. Moreover, it is a faith that bears the fruit of righteousness just as seed that is sown on good soil produces an abundant harvest.

The faith that Jesus is seeking from his followers is evident from his encounter with a rich young man (Matt. 19:13–30; Mark 10:17–31; Luke 18:18–29). This man came to Jesus with the question, "Teacher, what good thing must I do to get eternal life?" (Matt. 19:16). Jesus responded by telling him to obey the commandments. Jesus named some of these commandments and concluded with the comprehensive command, "Love your neighbor as yourself." The young man protested that he had done all these things. "What do I still lack?" Jesus answered, "If you want to be perfect, go, sell your possessions and give to the poor, and you will have treasure in heaven. Then come, follow me" (v. 21).

With this answer Jesus is seeking to cultivate faith in himself as Israel's Lord and Savior. He is asking the young man to "follow me." This young man had faith in Moses and the law, but that faith must now give way to faith in Jesus Christ. And this faith must be what faith must always be, a living, active, and obedient faith. The young man must follow Jesus. His faith must be an active trust in Messiah and the truth of his word. This is the kind of faith that gives access to the kingdom of God.

Jesus responded to the initial question by saying "If you want to enter life, obey the commandments." With these words Jesus was not endorsing a misguided effort to earn the reward of eternal life by the merit of good works. He was simply reiterating what was true under Moses and the law, what was true under the old covenant. The Lord says in Leviticus 18:5, "Keep my decrees and laws, for the man who obeys them will live by them. I am the Lord." It is clear from the context of verse 5 that the obedience required is the obedience of faith, the obedience that comes from faith. The Lord asks his people not to follow the practices of the

Egyptians or the practices of the Canaanites, but to follow him because he is their covenant Lord. Neither Leviticus 18:5 nor our Lord are promoting the merit of works. They are simply asking for the covenantal love and loyalty—the faith and faithfulness—that the Lord has always asked from his people.

As the conversation proceeds, two things become clear. First, faith in God as required under the old covenant is now faith in Jesus Christ because Jesus is the Son of God and Israel's Messiah. Second, faith in Jesus Christ, no less than faith in God under the old covenant, must be a living and active faith.

Sadly, the young man was not prepared to believe with this kind of faith. He was not prepared to part with his wealth, and so he went away sad. His obedience under the old covenant may have been sincere, but it was not the obedience of faith and therefore he did not respond positively to the gospel Jesus now proclaimed. Neither obedience without faith, nor faith without obedience will justify or save.

In the sequel to this encounter, however, it becomes evident that the faith of the disciples is a living and active faith. Peter says, "We have left everything to follow you! What then will there be for us?" (v. 27). Jesus promises his disciples nothing less than eternal life (v. 29). Eternal life is not the reward for meritorious achievement. Eternal life is the inheritance that is promised to faith, faith that is true and genuine, faith that is living and active, faith that is prepared to leave everything in order to follow Jesus.

Jesus is calling his disciples to a penitent and obedient faith. He is calling them to an enduring and persevering faith. He says, "If you love me, you will obey what I command" (John 14:15). Hebrews 5:9 says that Jesus "became the source of eternal salvation for all who obey him." His disciples will run into deception, insult, ridicule, opposition, and persecution, but Jesus makes this promise to them: "He who stands firm to the end will be saved" (Matt. 24:13).

When Jesus commissions his disciples to disciple the nations of the world, he tells them to do two things. First, they must call sinners to a baptism of repentance for the forgiveness of sins. They must call the nations of the world to repentance because a day is coming when God will come in judgment and the impenitent will not survive that day. And second, they must teach the nations to obey everything that Jesus has commanded (Matt. 28:20). In our evangelism practice today we stress faith alone, the one thing that Jesus does not expressly mention in the Great Commission. And we neglect the two things that he does mention, repentance and obedience.

For many people today it is inconceivable that calling nations to obey the commands of Jesus is evangelism, or that teaching our children to love Jesus and to obey his commands is evangelism. Many would call that justification by works and would condemn it roundly. James would also call it justification by works, and he would commend that kind of evangelism to us! Paul says in his letter to the Romans, the letter that teaches justification without the works of the law, that his task as an evangelist was to call the nations to the obedience that comes from faith (Rom. 1:5; 15:18; 16:26). Paul really understood what the Great Commission evangelism mandate was all about—teaching the nations to observe all that Jesus has commanded.

Our Lord in the New Testament, just as the Psalms and the Prophets in the Old Testament, makes a distinction between the righteous and the wicked. The righteous are not those who have simply received the imputed active obedience of Christ by faith. The righteous are those who have responded to the gospel call as defined in the Great Commission with faith, repentance, and obedience. The wicked are those who persevere in ungodliness. Paul says in Romans 1:17 that the righteous will live by faith. They will be saved in the Day of Judgment. In the next verse, verse 18, he says that on that same day the wrath of God will be revealed from heaven against the ungodliness and wickedness of men who suppress the truth by their wickedness. Jesus makes this distinction between the righteous and the wicked in Matthew 25, and describes the righteous as those who show mercy. In the Day of Judgment they will receive mercy. They need mercy because like all human beings they have sinned and their sins must be forgiven.

This is not the first time that Jesus makes this kind of dis-

tinction. He also makes it in the parable of the weeds in Matthew
13:24–30, 36–43. The weeds are those who cause sin and do evil,
and they will be destroyed in the fiery furnace. The wheat are the
righteous who will shine in the kingdom of their father. They will
be justified and saved in the Day of Judgment. The same distinction is made in the parable of the net found in the same chapter. The net hauls in both the good fish and the bad. In the final
judgment the angels will come and separate the wicked from the
righteous (v. 49). The wicked will be lost, but the righteous will be
saved.

The righteous mentioned in the preceding passages who will
be saved are not sinless persons, or persons who have had the active obedience of Christ imputed to them. They are sinners who
have confessed their sins and have turned from them in repentance. Daily they pray the Lord's Prayer and ask for the forgiveness
of their sins. They are righteous not because they are sinless but
because they are penitent. They are righteous because they love
the Lord who has forgiven their sin, and they seek to please him by
walking with him in obedience. As Jesus teaches in John 5:24, because they have believed in him they have crossed over from death
to life and have the promise of eternal life. Jesus goes on to say in
verse 29 that on the Day of Judgment the dead will rise from their
graves. "Those who have done good will rise to live, and those who
have done evil will rise to be condemned."

It has become apparent by now that in the proclamation of
the gospel, our Lord makes justification and salvation contingent
upon obedience. Evildoers will be destroyed, but the righteous will
enter into eternal life. There are several passages in the gospels
where this point is made quite expressly in an unmistakable way.
Jesus makes the forgiveness of our sins contingent upon our readiness to forgive those who have wronged us. Jesus says, "For if you
forgive men when they sin against you, your heavenly Father will
also forgive you. But if you do not forgive men their sins, your
Father will not forgive your sins" (Matt. 6:14, 15). The same teaching is found in Mark 11:25. It is also found at the conclusion of the
parable of the unmerciful servant. The master passes judgment on

the unmerciful servant and says, "This is how my heavenly Father will treat each of you unless you forgive your brother from your heart" (Matt. 18:35). These examples are striking because forgiveness belongs to the very essence of justification. Justification is the forgiveness of sins. Unless you are prepared to forgive, you will not be justified in the judgment of God.

Toward the end of the Sermon on the Mount Jesus says, "Every tree that does not bear good fruit is cut down and thrown into the fire" (Matt. 7:19). "Not everyone who says to me, 'Lord, Lord,' will enter the kingdom of heaven, but only he who does the will of my Father who is in heaven" (v. 21). In this verse we come very close to what James says in 2:14–26. Faith without works is dead. Only a living and active faith will justify. You must not only hear the word but you must do the will of the Father in heaven.

In Matthew 12:36, 37, Jesus says, "But I tell you that men will have to give account on the Day of Judgment for every careless word they have spoken. For by your words you will be acquitted, and by your words you will be condemned." This verse is talking about justification because it is talking about acquittal in the Day of Judgment. The Greek word for "acquitted" is the same word that is translated elsewhere in the New Testament as "justified." As noted previously, this is the other place in the gospels where the word "justify" is used in the Pauline forensic-soteric sense. Literally the verse says, "By your words you will be justified." Jesus is saying either you will be justified by your words or you will be condemned by them. This is justification by works ("words" are "works"), and it is in the teaching of our Lord. This is the closest grammatical parallel we have in the gospels to the teaching of James 2:24, "You see that a person is justified by what he does and not by faith alone."

Jesus tells the parable of the Good Samaritan in response to the question, "What must I do to inherit eternal life?" (Luke 10:25–28). Jesus asks what is written in the law and receives the answer, love the Lord your God and love your neighbor as yourself. "'You have answered correctly,' Jesus replied, 'Do this and you will live.'" At the end of the parable Jesus commends the example of the Good Samaritan and says, "Go and do likewise." Here Jesus is not teaching justification by the merit of good works. The element of showing mercy is similar to what we have in Matthew 25 and in James 2. The Good Samaritan furnishes a good example of faith working by love (Gal. 5:6). This is justification by faith, and this is the kind of faith that justifies.

Jesus says in Matthew 16:27, "For the Son of Man is going to come in his Father's glory with his angels, and then he will reward each person according to what he has done." This is really a quotation from Psalm 62:12. Paul quotes these same words in Romans 2:6. The reward is more than a higher degree of blessing in the kingdom. The immediate context and the broader context of the teaching of our Lord show that the reward is eternal life itself. It is a judgment according to works and a reward according to works.

The point in all of this is that Jesus makes justification contingent upon obedience. The Lord God justifies the righteous and condemns the wicked. But now, how is that good news for sinners? Isn't the gospel precisely this, that Jesus saves sinners? In the words of Paul, the good news is that God justifies the wicked (Rom. 4:5). Doesn't Jesus say in Matthew 9:13 that he has not come to call the righteous, but sinners?

The answer to this question is found in Luke 5:32, the passage that is parallel to Matthew 9:13. In Luke 5:32 Jesus says, "I have not come to call the righteous, but sinners *to repentance*." Jesus calls sinners to repentance. In the familiar parable of the Pharisee and the Tax Collector, it is the sinner (the wicked person) who is justified (Luke 18:9–14). He confesses his sin and is genuinely penitent. In this he demonstrates a genuine righteousness. The Pharisee claims to be righteous. He does works of the law and has no sin to confess—at least in his own mind. The Lord does not justify this sinner on the ground of his works of the law. Jesus justifies the sinner who confesses his sin and repents of it. The good news of the gospel is not that Jesus forgives sinners who persevere in their ungodliness, but that he forgives sinners who repent.

So it is, also, in the conversion of Zacchaeus (Luke 19:1–9).

Here is a sinner who believes and is saved; but he is not saved in his sin. He repents and proves his repentance by his deeds. He makes restitution for what he has taken unjustly. Zacchaeus comes to Jesus with a penitent and obedient faith and is justified and saved.

Jesus, Paul, and James

At this point it is not difficult to see how the public ministry of our Lord lays the foundation for what Paul and James have to say about justification. Jesus comes into the world as the ultimate prophet calling Israel to repentance and offering himself as a sacrifice for sin. Through faith in himself and through repentance Jesus leads his disciples into possession of eternal life. He leads them through the narrow gate and sets them on the narrow way that leads to eternal life (Matt. 7:13, 14). This is the Way of Holiness described in Isaiah 35:8–10. He assures his disciples that in the face of insult, opposition, and persecution, they must persevere in this way. The Lord will never leave or forsake his own. They are justified now—the Lord has forgiven their sins and they are in the right with God—and they will be justified on the Day of Judgment.

Paul carries this same message to the Gentiles, the message of justification and salvation through faith in Jesus who died for our sins and was raised for our justification. Jews who cling to Moses and do works of the law in order to be justified and saved do not know the way of faith. They do not know Jesus. As Paul teaches in his letter to the Galatians, telling the Gentiles that they must submit to Moses and the provisions of the old covenant is a gospel that is no gospel. It is an accursed anti-gospel because it leads the Gentiles away from Jesus Christ. It takes away any hope of salvation because it makes justification dependent upon works of the law. It makes justification dependent on one's own performance, on something in which we can boast, instead of wholly and exclusively dependent on Jesus.

According to Paul in Galatians the way for pious Jews to be faithful to Moses is to say farewell to Moses. Like the Gentiles they must also cling to Jesus because Moses wrote about Jesus and leads us to Jesus. Paul calls both Jew and Gentile to repentance and faith in Jesus with the assurance that those who believe will be justified and saved. Faith is a living, active, and obedient faith.

James writes from the same perspective to believers who have come to repentance and faith. He warns them that faith alone, faith that does not come to expression in obedience to our Lord, in love for our neighbors, and in works of mercy, is not the kind of faith that saves. It is dead faith. James exhorts his readers in chapter 1 to be doers of the word and not hearers only.

Jesus, Paul, and James all make justification and salvation contingent upon a penitent and obedient faith. All of this has nothing to do with justification or salvation on the ground of the merit of good works. Faith receives what is promised. Living, active, penitent, and obedient faith can only receive what is promised, and what is promised is pure grace. Jesus died and rose again to take away the guilt of sin and to destroy its power. He recreates us in his own image so that we can bring glory to God on the earth by reflecting his righteousness and holiness. In this way God saves us and leads us into possession of eternal life. We are saved by grace through faith.

Just as the ministry of James and Paul is grounded in that of our Lord, so also the teaching of our Lord is rooted and grounded in what has gone before. Therefore we turn now to the Old Testament to appreciate how the gospel of justification by grace through faith is unfolded in the old covenant.

CHAPTER 4

Justification Under the Old Covenant

T he heart of the Old Testament lies in the Book of Exodus, and in the establishment of the old covenant at Mt. Sinai. There the Lord formed his people into a nation, the first of the nations to be discipled into his kingdom. Covenant defines a divinely, sovereignly, and unilaterally established relationship of union and communion between the Lord and his people in the bonds of mutual love and faithfulness. The Mosaic covenant established at Mt. Sinai regulated the life of the covenant community and the lives of God's people from that time to the advent of Christ and the establishment of the new covenant. The question for us now is, how were sinners justified and saved under this old covenant?

We read about the establishment of the old covenant in Exodus, Leviticus, Numbers, and Deuteronomy. The rest of the Old Testament tells us about the life of Israel under the old covenant. Moses wrote Genesis as a preface to Exodus and as an introduction to the old covenant. In Genesis we learn where human beings came from and what their calling in the world is. We learn how sin entered into human experience and what the consequences of sin are for the human condition. Genesis also introduces us to God's announced will to save a people for his own treasured possession.

Our Lord's intention in all of this is to have at the end of human history what he intended to have from the very beginning. His purpose in creating the human race cannot and will not fail. The Lord will realize this goal in spite of the entrance of sin, condemnation, and death into the world. In this chapter we will consider justification before the establishment of the Mosaic covenant, and then justification under the Mosaic covenant in the law, the prophets, and the Psalms (wisdom literature).

Justification Before the Mosaic Covenant

We can begin where human history begins, with Adam. We will go on from there to consider the examples of Noah and Abraham. Of course, Adam did not come into the world as a sinner but as righteous and holy, and therefore at the beginning justification was not a soteric experience. We know that Adam was righteous and holy because he was created in the image of a righteous and holy God. Paul makes this point expressly in Ephesians 4:24 and Colossians 3:10. There Paul says that now, through the power of Jesus' death and resurrection, we are recreated in the image of God in righteousness and holiness and in the knowledge of the truth. What holds first place in the re-creation held first place in the original creation. Adam was created, not simply without sin, but righteous and holy. Romans 5 shows us that sin entered the world of human experience through the sin of Adam in eating the forbidden fruit. Therefore prior to that time Adam was without sin and did not need to be justified from sin.

Since Adam was created righteous and holy he was just in the judgment of his Creator from the very beginning of his existence. That is to say, he was created as a justified man. He did not have to become righteous or holy. He was not created morally neutral or indifferent. He did not have to do something to become just in the judgment of God. He did not have to do anything in order to earn or achieve the status of a justified person, or to enter into a justified state. We read nothing of that kind in Genesis 1, 2, or 3.

The Lord planted two trees in the Garden of Eden, the Tree of Life and the Tree of the Knowledge of Good and Evil. The Tree of Life symbolized the life that he received from his Creator. He was made to be a living creature. The Tree of Life also held out before him the promise of life, or the promise of eschatological blessing and all that pertained to it. We can infer this from the nature of the eschatological blessing given to redeemed sinners under the new covenant, and from the experience of Enoch, the seventh from Adam, recorded in Genesis 5:23, 24 and Hebrews 11:5, 6.

The relation God sustained to Adam was covenantal in character. It was a relationship of union and communion in the bonds of mutual love and faithfulness. All biblical covenants have these two sides, promise and obligation; and this was true before the fall into sin as well as after the fall. All of the benefits Adam received and would receive from God were his by gift and by promise; and the gifts and promises of God are always received by faith. Adam could do nothing to earn or merit eternal life, but he could forfeit life by his unbelief and disobedience. That brings us to the obligation side of the covenant. The other tree in the Garden was the Tree of Knowledge, and God told Adam not to eat from this Tree. The penalty for disobedience was death for him and for his posterity. It is clear that Adam was not asked to do something in order to earn or merit the right to eternal life. He was told not to do something lest he forfeit the life to which he was otherwise entitled by the gift and promise of God. Adam could eat from every other tree of the garden, and so there was no reason not to eat of this tree except for the fact that God told him not to eat of it. Thus obedience to this command was a pure act of faith, the obedience that flows from faith.

There were other things that God told Adam to do. He was under obligation to reproduce his own kind and to rule over the world that God had created to be his home. We call this the cultural mandate. The Tree of Knowledge was there to remind Adam that in all of this cultural activity he was responding to the word of God. Obedience to the cultural mandate was a matter of faith in God and faithfulness to God and his word. The obedience of faith (both the obedience that flows from faith and the obedience that is faith) was focused in the command not to eat of the Tree of Knowledge. Adam was to live by every word that proceeds from the mouth of God (Deut. 8:3), and that is to say he was to live by faith. The issue in the temptation was not whether he could or would earn the right to eternal life, but whether he would receive life as a gift by faith or perish in unbelief and disobedience.

Consider now the fact that Adam was created holy and righteous, without sin. He was the original just man. Faith for Adam was a living and active faith, a matter of discharging the cultural mandate. This was the obedience of faith. Along the path of faith and obedience the Lord was leading him into confirmed righteousness and eternal life. In other words, Adam was created as a just man to live by faith. The method of justification for Adam is exactly what it is for Paul as described in Romans 1:17. "The righteous will live by faith." Adam was a righteous man who would live by faith. Of course there is this major difference between Adam and those who came after him: Justification for us now takes place after the fall into sin and on the background of sin and condemnation. Therefore justification is not only forensic but also soteric. Justification now includes the forgiveness of sin, and faith is faith in the blood of Jesus. But the basic structure is the same: the righteous live by faith. It is true both before and after the fall that the righteous live by faith.

Adam was created in the image of God as a just man who would live by faith. Through the power of Jesus' death and resurrection sinners are re-created in the image of God in righteousness and holiness (Eph. 4:24; Col. 3:10). In Christ we become righteous men who live now and forever by faith. Through Christ rather than through Adam we attain to that confirmation in righteousness and to the eternal life that was held out before him in promise as his eschatological destiny. "For if, by the trespass of the one man, death reigned through that one man, how much more will those who receive God's abundant provision of grace and of the gift of righteousness reign in life through the one man, Jesus Christ" (Rom. 5:17). The next verse, verse 18, shows that justification by faith brings life.

If Adam had believed God and acted accordingly, his destiny would have been comparable to what we read concerning Enoch in Genesis 5:21–24. Enoch did not experience death as we know it. "Enoch walked with God; then he was no more, because God took him away." Hebrews 11:5 tells us, "By faith Enoch was taken from this life, so that he did not experience death; he could not be found, because God had taken him away. For before he was taken, he was commended as one who pleased God." Enoch shows the similarity in the method of justification before the fall and after the fall. That method is summarized by Paul in the words of Habakkuk

2:4, "The righteous will live by faith." Enoch was a righteous man who lived and lived forever by faith. He was justified by faith.

From the justification of Adam we can move on to the justification of Noah. Genesis 6:5 says, "The Lord saw how great man's wickedness on the earth had become, and that every inclination of the thoughts of his heart was only evil all the time." God's good creation had become a cesspool of iniquity. However, in the midst of this cesspool of iniquity there is a notable exception—Noah. Verse 6 describes Noah as "a righteous man, blameless among the people of his time." That is the first point we need to observe, that Noah was a righteous man.

The second point is simply that Noah lived. From time to time the Lord brings reformation to his church, but not always in the same way. In the days of Noah reformation came by way of judgment. The only thing comparable is the judgment to come at the end of the present age (2 Pet. 3:6, 7). Therefore the story of Noah brings us into the sphere of justification—what will happen to us in the Day of Judgment.

Why did Noah live? Why did he survive the flood? Did his own righteousness keep him alive? Hardly! The rains that came down and the floods that came up were totally indifferent to Noah and his righteousness. Actually Noah was a sinner like every other human being that has been born in the natural way. He, together with his family, deserved to be swept away by the waters of judgment. But Noah lived because God preserved this man. God intervened in human history to save Noah and to save the lives of his family as well. Noah survived the judgment of God because God himself provided a way of escape—the ark. To survive in the judgment of God is precisely what we mean by justification. Instead of dying in God's just judgment we are forgiven and accepted by God. We live! To say that Noah lived is to say that he was justified. Noah, the righteous man, lives. He is justified.

The third observation we have to make about Noah is, of course, that Noah lived *by faith*. Noah was a righteous man who stood head and shoulders above his contemporaries, but he did not stand tall enough to keep his head above the floodwaters. Suppose

Noah had protested his innocence, his blamelessness, his holiness, would that have stopped the rain? Of course not! Noah had no way in himself, no resources in himself, to save himself. He was saved because God provided a way of escape. Faith in God and faith in his word saved Noah. Genesis 6:8 tells us that Noah found favor in the eyes of the Lord. He became a beneficiary of the un-merited grace of God. God spoke from heaven and warned Noah of the flood that would come—the judgment. It sounds fantastic to think that such a flood could come; but even more fantastic was the command to build an ark on dry land! What a ridiculous thing to do when the sky is perpetually blue and the prediction is for nothing but fair weather ahead.

No doubt Noah's contemporaries regarded Noah as some sort of religious fanatic, some kind of religious nut, the same way Christians today are regarded as naïve and fanatical for believing that there is going to be a final judgment some day, but Noah kept hammering away on the ark. Noah believed God and he acted on his faith. His faith was a living, active, and obedient faith, and here we see what is the very essence of Noah's righteousness. His was not simply the righteousness of duty performed according to pre-scribed rules. His was faith-righteousness. He believed God and acted accordingly. Noah believed in God and he believed what God said. Therefore he built the ark when God told him to build it. When the Day of Judgment came, Noah the righteous man lived by faith. He was saved from condemnation by God's grace through faith. "By faith Noah, when warned about things not yet seen, in holy fear built an ark to save his family. By his faith he condemned the world and became heir of the righteousness that comes by faith" (Heb. 11:17). This is the truth that Paul saw so clearly revealed in the Old Testament both by word and by ex-ample. "The righteous will live by faith."

From Noah we can move on to Abraham. Abraham figures significantly in the doctrine of justification because of the appeal that both Paul and James make to his experience. For Paul the justification of Abraham demonstrates that justification is by faith and not by works of the law. Abraham was justified long before the Law was promulgated on Mt. Sinai, and even before he was circumcised. Circumcision was a shorthand way of referring to the whole Mosaic system of law. Abraham is justified by faith, and that is the same way in which believers under the new covenant are justified today.

Sometimes we represent the difference between justification by faith and justification by works as the difference between justification by believing (faith alone, faith without works) and justification by doing (works alone, works without faith, or even works in addition to faith). This is not what Paul has in view when he contrasts justification by faith with justification by works. Paul's appeal to Abraham shows that the difference is really the difference between faith in the promises of God over against resort to the provisions of the Mosaic covenant. Justification by faith under the new covenant requires abandoning the old Mosaic covenant because that covenant is now obsolete and passing away (Heb. 8:13). The difference lies in the progress of redemptive revelation and the advent of Jesus Christ in history to accomplish redemption.

For James the example of Abraham shows that the faith by which we are justified is not a dead faith, but a living and obedient faith. Again, believing is not set over against doing as antithetical to doing. James says that the faith by which Abraham was justified was a faith that was prepared to offer up Isaac at the command of the Lord God. Abraham was ready to do that when he could not see how the promise of God could be fulfilled except through Isaac as his living heir. The act of Abraham was an act of faith. In Hebrews 11:7 the author refers to the same act of faith. "By faith Abraham, when God tested him, offered Isaac as a sacrifice." This chapter also refers to the fact that by faith Abraham left his home in obedience to the Lord "even though he did not know where he was going." Again, by faith Abraham fathered Isaac when that was physically impossible for him and his wife. He believed the promise that God made to him.

The Scriptures present Abraham to us as a righteous man. The Lord commanded him to "walk before me and be blameless," and that is what Abraham did (Gen. 17:1). In Genesis 18:19 God says, "For I have chosen him, so that he will direct his children and his household after him to keep the way of the Lord by doing what is right and just, so that the Lord will bring about for Abraham what he has promised him." Abraham is a man who did what was right and just. He was a faithful covenant keeper. In Genesis 26:1–6 God renews for Isaac the promises he made to Abraham. These promises will be fulfilled "because Abraham obeyed me and kept my requirements, my commands, my decrees and my laws." The picture that emerges from all of this is that Abraham is a God-fearing man who walked in the ways of the Lord. We do not need to think of him as without sin, but the Lord forgave his sin and Abraham did not live a sinful lifestyle. Here was a righteous man who lived by faith. It is the same pattern that we see in Adam before the fall, in Enoch and Noah after the fall, and that we now see in the new covenant. It is the pattern that Paul commends to us in Romans 4:12 when talking about justification. We must "walk in the footsteps of the faith that our father Abraham had before he was circumcised."

Sometimes the discussion of Abraham's justification focuses on the question, when was Abraham justified? Was it in Genesis 12, or 15, or 17, or in chapter 22 when he offered Isaac? The point in Genesis, as well as for Paul and James, is not so much *when* as *how*. Abraham is justified—he is in a right relationship with God—not on the basis of any meritorious accomplishment but by faith. The man who believes in God, who believes God's word and acts accordingly, is in a right relationship with the Lord. He is not under condemnation and will not come into condemnation but is justified and will be saved in the Day of Judgment. "The righteous will live by faith."

Justification under the Mosaic Covenant

The Adamic, Noahic, and Abrahamic covenants are all pre-paratory for what happened at Mt. Sinai. There God formed his people into a nation and established his covenant with them. The question before us now is, how were God's people justified under the provisions of this covenant? To answer this question we will consider in turn the three parts of the Hebrew Old Testament, the law, the prophets, and the Psalms (wisdom literature). In the next chapter we consider the fourth part of our four-part Bible, the New Testament.

An outstanding feature of this Sinai covenant is the detailed laws that God gave his people in order to regulate their lives. We should not think of these laws as a set of rules that have to be kept in order to merit the reward of eternal life. Nor did God give his law in order to demonstrate to Israelites that there was no hope in trying to save themselves by their good works because they could not perform perfect obedience anyway. We have to see the first five books of the Bible as the gospels of the old covenant. They correspond to the first four books of the new covenant, Matthew, Mark, Luke, and John. They tell the story of God's powerful and supernatural work to save his people from sin and condemnation in Egypt corresponding to the work of Christ revealed in our four gospels. They show God's people how to enjoy and maintain covenant fellowship with the living and true God who has chosen them to be his people, his treasured possession.

The sin of Adam had left the human race with two problems: the guilt of sin and the corruption of sin. The guilt of sin rendered us all liable to the punishment of eternal condemnation and death. The corruption of sin made it impossible for us to please God, to do his will, or to have fellowship with him. The laws of the Mosaic covenant are designed to solve both of these problems. That is why the Mosaic covenant is a gracious covenant. Like all the great historical covenants, the Mosaic covenant is a covenant of grace, pure and simple.

The Lord God deals with the guilt of sin by revealing his will to forgive sin. Nothing demonstrates the gracious character of the Mosaic covenant more than this, the revelation of God's will to forgive sin. This is the great purpose served by the sacrificial system outlined in the Mosaic Law and described for us in the Book of Hebrews. The tabernacle and temple were set up so that priests could offer sacrifices daily for their own sins and for the sins of the people. Then there are the sacrifices of the great Day of

Atonement. The message was that without the shedding of blood there is no remission of sin (Heb. 9:22).

The Lord God deals with the corruption and power of sin by teaching his people how to live. The Lord taught his people how to avoid the wickedness of surrounding nations. That is the point of Leviticus 18:5 in the context of verses 1–4. God's people are not to live like the Egyptians or like the Canaanites. They are to live and prosper the way the Lord teaches them in his law. "Keep my decrees and laws, for the man who obeys them will live by them. I am the Lord." That is simply to say they are to live by faith in God, by a living faith that is an obedient faith.

Many of the commandments are in a negative form, to counteract the influence and power of sin in the world. God taught his people how to live in harmony and fellowship with one another and with their God. He taught them what to do when the harmony was broken and how to restore it. He taught them how to live happy and productive lives in total dependence on the goodness of their Father in heaven who promised to send seedtime and harvest, sunshine and rain. In other words, he taught them in his law how to be righteous men who would live by faith. God would be glorified as his image bearers and covenant partners reflected his righteousness in the earth.

To summarize, how are sinners justified under the Mosaic covenant? They confess their sins and seek forgiveness from the Lord by the faithful use of the sacrificial system. The ministry of the priests assures them that their sins are forgiven. They are justified. By that same faith they walk with the Lord in obedience to his commands. They walk in the footsteps of the faith of their father, Abraham. They are not without sin, but their sin is pardoned. They sin, but they do not give themselves over to a sinful lifestyle. These people are called the righteous in Israel and they are set over against the wicked who have contempt for the Lord and his ways. They are the righteous who live by faith.

The sad story of the Old Testament is the story of how God's people refused to be a holy and righteous people and how they refused to live by faith. Instead, they turned away from the

Lord in unbelief and disobedience. Instead of a righteous people living by faith they became an ungodly people who would perish in their unbelief. Moses says in Deuteronomy 9:23, 24, "And when the Lord sent you out from Kadesh Barnea, he said, 'Go up and take possession of the land I have given you.' But you rebelled against the command of the Lord your God. You did not trust him or obey him. You have been rebellious against the Lord ever since I have known you." Hebrews 3:18, 19 repeats the same thought concerning the same episode. It is a pattern of unbelief and disobedience that is repeated throughout Israel's history.

For this reason the Lord sent prophets to his people. The prophets point out the evil that is being done in the nation, and they call the people to repentance. If the people repent and turn to the Lord, the Lord will forgive their sin and receive them again as his people. "Repent! Turn away from all your offenses; then sin will not be your downfall. Rid yourselves of all the offenses you have committed, and get a new heart and a new spirit. Why will you die, O house of Israel? For I take no pleasure in the death of anyone, declares the Sovereign Lord. Repent and live!" (Ezek. 18:30–32). Repentance is unto the forgiveness of sin. The penitent will be justified and saved. They will live and live forever. But Israel refuses to repent and be saved.

Nevertheless, Israel does seek justification in its own way, namely, by works of the law. In Isaiah 1 the prophet describes Israel as a "sinful nation, a people loaded with guilt, a brood of evildoers, children given to corruption!" Yet they continue to offer sacrifices, and the Lord responds by saying, "'The multitude of your sacrifices—what are they to me?' says the Lord. 'I have more than enough of burnt offerings, of rams and the fat of fattened animals; I have no pleasure in the blood of bulls and lambs and goats.'" These sacrifices are what Paul calls "works of the law" designed to cover up gross transgressions, and the Lord will have none of it. Paul makes the same point in Romans 1, 2, and 3 when he calls for repentance and says that we are justified by faith and not by works of the law. This is what Isaiah is talking about in 64:6 when he says, "all our righteous acts are like filthy rags." Micah 6 deals with the same problem, as does Psalm 51:15–17 also.

The prophets of the old covenant teach justification by faith, faith that issues in repentance and obedience. This is where Paul learned his doctrine of justification by faith and why he quotes a prophet to sum up his own doctrine. "The righteous will live by his faith" (Hab. 2:4). The Hebrew word for "faith" used in this verse also means "faithfulness," and this is the reading given in the margin of the New International Version. The faith by which the righteous live is a penitent and obedient faith. Paul says in Romans 3:21, "But now a righteousness from God, apart from law, has been made known, to which the Law and the Prophets testify." Paul sees his own doctrine of justification by faith as continuous with what we find in the Mosaic laws and in the ministry of the prophets.

The Law and the Prophets teach justification by a living, active, and penitent faith. So also does the third division of the Old Testament, the Psalms or the Wisdom Literature. As you read the Book of Psalms you realize that a profound distinction is made between the righteous and the wicked. It begins in Psalm 1 and sets the tone for the whole book. The wicked will be destroyed, but the righteous will be blessed. The righteous are covenant keepers who are in a right relationship with the Lord. Their sins are forgiven and therefore they are not under condemnation. The Lord receives and accepts them as his beloved people. They are justified saints. They are the righteous who live by faith.

Psalm 15 asks, "Lord, who may dwell in your sanctuary? Who may live on your holy hill?" The answer is, "He whose walk is blameless and who does what is righteous, who speaks the truth from his heart." We should not say that no person meets this qualification, only Christ whose active obedience is then imputed to us. That thought renders the Psalm meaningless to the people who first sang it. This idea is not in the Psalm and it is not the point of the Psalm. Nor, on the other hand, does the Psalm teach justification and salvation by the merit of good works. The point of the Psalm is that the man who keeps covenant with the Lord, who does what is right in the eyes of the Lord, and who walks in the footsteps of father Abraham, is a man of faith. He is the righteous man who lives by faith. Our churches today have many such people as members, and if we don't we are in very, very serious trouble!

This righteous man of Psalm 15 is not without sin, but his sin is forgiven. This theme of forgiveness is developed so beautifully in Psalm 51. The Psalmist confesses his sin and cries out for mercy. 2 Samuel 12:13 tells us that David confessed his sin and Nathan assures him that the Lord has taken his sin away. That is justification. He pleads with the Lord to create a new heart within so that he can teach transgressors by word and example the ways of the Lord. This is sanctification. Justification and sanctification are inseparable in the application of redemption.

The message of the Psalms is justification by faith. The man who seeks pardon from the Lord and who serves the Lord with gladness is in a right relationship with the Lord. The Lord will deliver him in the final judgment and will lead him into everlasting life. "You have made known to me the path of life; you will fill me with joy in your presence, with eternal pleasures at your right hand" (Ps. 16:11).

The Proverbs give us insight into the wisdom of God's law. The wise man is the man who pays attention to God's law and puts it into practice. This is the man who stands in a right relationship with the Lord and who can expect to prosper now and forever. "My son, do not forget my teaching, but keep my commands in your heart, for they will prolong your life many years and bring you prosperity" (Prov. 3:1, 2). This is not justification or salvation by works as is evident from verses 5, 6. "Trust in the Lord with all your heart and lean not on your own understanding; in all your ways acknowledge him, and he will make your paths straight." The man who trusts the Lord with all his heart (faith) is the man who has the commands of the Lord in his heart.

Proverbs 12:28 says, "In the way of righteousness there is life; along that path is immortality." The purpose of this Proverb is not to teach us that our justification and salvation depend on the merit of our good works. The purpose of the Proverb is to encourage us to walk in the way of righteousness and along the path that leads to eternal life. When we read Proverbs 12:28 we have to remember the words of our Lord in the Sermon on the Mount, in Matthew 7:13, 14. "Enter through the narrow gate. For wide is the gate and broad is the road that leads to destruction, and many enter through it. But small is the gate and narrow the road that leads to life, and only a few find it." Jesus is not teaching justification by the merit of works. Both Proverbs 12:28 and our Lord are talking about the way of faith, what Isaiah 35:8 calls the "Way of Holiness."

We find the same gospel throughout the Old Testament and throughout the New Testament. The righteous will live, not by the merit of their works, but by faith, and this faith is a living, active, penitent, and obedient faith. But under the old covenant God's people refused to be the people God called them to be. Something was missing, and what was missing was Jesus Christ, the incarnate Son of God. He had not yet been born. He had not yet died nor was he risen from the dead. That brings us to a consideration of justification under the new covenant, justification in the blood of Jesus.

CHAPTER 5

Justification Under the New Covenant

Actually we have already considered justification under the new covenant in our study of justification according to James, Paul, and our Lord and we do not need to cover the same ground again. Our focus now is on the experience of justification among the people of God. How do people make the transition from wrath to grace, or from condemnation and death to justification and life? How do they get justified, how do they stay justified, and how do they know they are justified?

The Conversion of Sinners

The Lord God had been wonderfully good to his people, Israel. The Lord had liberated them from slavery in Egypt under the leadership of Moses. He not only gave them life, he also taught them how to live. The Mosaic Law is the evidence of God's goodness to Israel and the recorded demonstration of his saving grace and love. However, God's people rebelled against their Father in heaven and so the Lord sent prophets to call them to repentance, but without success. The last of the old covenant prophets was John the Baptist who announced that judgment was at hand. Then in one last dramatic effort the Lord sent his own Son as the ultimate prophet to preach repentance and the forgiveness of sin. Instead of trusting and obeying, God's people killed Jesus.

Jesus began his ministry as the ultimate prophet and brought this ministry to a climax as the ultimate priest. By his death and resurrection Jesus accomplished what the law was intended to do, but never could do. He made definitive atonement for sin as the ground of our forgiveness, our justification; and he destroyed the power and corruption of sin, laying the ground for the regeneration and sanctification of his people. In the words of Paul to Timothy,

Jesus destroyed death and brought life and immortality to light (2 Tim. 1:10). Following his resurrection Jesus ascended into heaven to reign as the ultimate king. Now Jesus sends his Holy Spirit to apply the benefits that he wrought for them by his death and resurrection. Now he is building his church as sinners are transformed into saints and become the righteous who live by faith.

What happens when sinners are converted? How is Christ building his church? In the beginning God created human beings for union and communion with himself, for covenant fellowship. Sin separates us from fellowship with God and alienates us from him. We become hostile to God. Therefore the initiative for restoration of that fellowship comes from God himself. That is his saving grace. Because of our separation from God, God comes to us with his grace from outside of us, in the preaching of his gospel.

The Lord commissions his church to preach the gospel, to proclaim the word of life. That commission is fulfilled in a variety of ways, some of them more formal that others. In any case, the word of the gospel strikes our ears, and the Holy Spirit accompanies that word with power according to the sovereign will and purpose of God. "Our gospel came to you not simply with words, but also with power, with the Holy Spirit and with deep conviction" (1 Thess. 1:5). The Spirit drives that word home to the heart. This is the teaching or the testimony of the Holy Spirit. "You have an anointing from the Holy One, and all of you know the truth" (1 John 2:20). The Holy Spirit also transforms the heart to receive the word. In Acts 16:14 the Lord opens Lydia's heart to respond to Paul's message. This is the regenerating work of the Holy Spirit, the new birth. At the same time the Holy Spirit takes up residence in us; he comes to live in us. Paul says in Romans 8:9 that the Holy Spirit lives in us so that we are activated, motivated, and controlled by the Holy Spirit. The presence of the Holy Spirit in us unites us to Christ because the Spirit is the Spirit of Christ. In Romans 8:9 Paul calls the Holy Spirit the Spirit of Christ, the same Spirit who raised Jesus from the dead. Because we have the Spirit of Christ, we have Christ in us. We are united to Christ and belong to him. Thus united to Christ we become the beneficiaries of all that

Christ has done for us by his death and resurrection. Specifically, we are justified—our sins are forgiven—and we are sanctified—recreated in the image of God in righteousness and holiness.

Regeneration, justification, adoption, and sanctification represent the promise side of the new covenant, and these promises are received by faith. According to Romans 10:14, 15, faith comes by hearing the word preached or proclaimed. What do we do when we preach the gospel, and what kind of response are we looking for?

First, we expose the sin of the sinners to whom we proclaim the gospel. We have to demonstrate by comparison of human behavior with the standards of the word of God that all have sinned and stand under the judgment of eternal condemnation and death. We do that in dependence upon the teaching and transforming power of the Holy Spirit. Second, we tell guilty sinners what God has done for us in Christ to save us from sin, condemnation, and death. This is simply the story of the Bible from Genesis to Revelation, but with a focus on the person and work of Jesus Christ, his death and resurrection. We explain who Jesus is, why he came, why he died for us, why he rose again, and why he is now ascended into heaven. Third, we plead with sinners to come to Jesus so that their sins can be forgiven. We teach them to come in the only way they can come, in repentance and faith. Faith and repentance are inseparably intertwined. It is impossible to turn to Jesus in faith without turning away from sin in repentance. When this preaching is accompanied by the power of the Holy Spirit, sinners do respond in repentance and faith. At this point they are converted. As directed in the Great Commission we baptize them with a baptism of repentance for the remission of sins. They are justified and saved.

Fourth, we teach these converted sinners to observe all that Jesus has commanded. This is also in fulfillment of the Great Commission and is integral to the evangelistic task of the church. Evangelism includes not only bringing sinners to the point of conversion but also getting them started walking on the path of righteousness, the Way of Holiness (Isa. 35:8). Fifth, we encourage God's people to persevere in this faith and to keep walking in the Way of Holiness no matter what obstacles, opposition, or discouragement they may meet along the way. And sixth, we assure these pilgrims that they are on the right path, and that the Lord will never leave or forsake them. Those who endure to the end will be saved because there is no condemnation now or ever for those who are in Christ Jesus (Rom. 8:1). Both perseverance and assurance are intimately tied in with the biblical doctrine of justification, and for that reason we need to reflect more fully on both of these graces in relation to justification.

Perseverance in Faith

The Bible teaches that we are justified by faith. That is, we enter into a right relationship with God through faith in Jesus Christ as Lord and Savior. Because of what Jesus has done for us in his death and resurrection, the Lord God forgives our sin and recreates us in righteousness and holiness. This faith by which we enter into this justified state is not a dead faith. It is inseparably intertwined with repentance. We cannot turn to Christ in faith without turning away from sin in repentance. Further, justifying faith is not a momentary act. It is not the act of a single moment. It is not a mathematical point without a time dimension. Justifying faith is an ongoing reality in the life of the believer. That is why the believer is called a believer. He believes and keeps on believing. We cannot say that we enter into a justified state by faith and then we remain in that state by works. We enter into a justified state by means of a living faith and we remain in a justified state by means of a living faith. This is to say that the sinner whose sin is forgiven and who has been transformed into the likeness of Christ—all by faith—perseveres in that faith and so remains in a right relationship with God.

Perseverance in faith is represented to us in Scripture as a gift from God. It is one of the gracious benefits that we receive from our union with Christ. Jesus tells us in John 10:27–29 that he knows who his sheep are and that he gives them eternal life. They follow Jesus and they will never perish. He says, "No one can snatch them out of my Father's hand." Paul gives this promise in 1 Corinthians 1:8, 9, "[God] will keep you strong to the end, so that you will be blameless on the day of our Lord Jesus Christ. God who has called you into fellowship with his Son Jesus Christ our Lord, is faithful." On the basis of this promise Paul offers this prayer in 1 Thessalonians 5:23, 24, "May your whole spirit, soul and body be kept blameless at the coming of our Lord Jesus Christ. The one who calls you is faithful and he will do it." In Philippians 1:6 Paul expresses his confidence "that he who began a good work in you will carry it on to completion until the day of Christ Jesus." Peter adds his testimony in 1 Peter 1:3–5. There he says that we have been born again into a living hope through the resurrection of Jesus Christ from the dead. We have an inheritance that can never perish, spoil, or fade. We are "shielded by God's power until the coming of the salvation that is ready to be revealed in the last time."

In all of these promises the end point in view is the Day of Judgment and the consummation of all things. Thus not even the intervention of the death in the experience of the believer can undo the promise that has been made. This is, of course, what Paul affirms in Romans 8:38, 39. Not even death itself can separate us from the love of God that is in Christ Jesus our Lord.

Of course, this promise of perseverance, like all of God's promises, must be received by faith, and saving faith is always a living and active faith. Therefore coupled with the promise of perseverance as a gift is the exhortation to persevere in faith and obedience to the Lord. The New Testament is filled with this kind of exhortation and encouragement. We see it very clearly in the book of Revelation and in the letters to the seven churches with which the book opens. For example, the exhortation to the church in Smyrna is, "Be faithful, even to the point of death, and I will give you the crown of life" (Rev. 2:10). Often the exhortation is coupled with a warning about the consequences of being unfaithful and falling away. First Corinthians 10:1–13 is a powerful example of this. Here Paul brings forward examples from the experience of the people of God under the old covenant. He says that these things were written down as examples for us on whom the fulfillment of the ages has come, that we should not make the same kind of mistakes they made and perish.

The whole book of Hebrews is written to Jews who have left Moses behind in order to follow Christ. It is one grand plea to them to persevere in that faith. They have not made a mistake by moving from the synagogue to the church. They are on the right track and they will not fail to enter into eternal life, so "hang in there!" The verse that is of special interest because of its direct connection to justification is Hebrews 10:36. "You need to persevere so that when you have done the will of God, you will receive what he has promised." This verse comes at the end of a chapter in which the author urges believers to draw near to God in full assurance of faith (v. 22). He urges them to hold unswervingly "to the hope we profess, for he who promised is faithful" (v. 23). He urges them to spur one another on "toward love and good deeds," and to encourage one another as they see the Day approaching (vs. 24, 25). Then comes a solemn warning about the day to come when the Lord will judge his people. Now we are clearly in the sphere of justification. Those who trample the blood of the covenant under foot and insult the Spirit of grace will not survive that judgment. "You need to persevere so that when you have done the will of God, you will receive what he has promised" (v. 36).

In verse 36 the author does not mention faith expressly, but he does mention it in both the preceding and following verses. What he expressly urges is perseverance in doing the will of God. Just as faith without works is dead, so works without faith are dead. The verse urges perseverance in a living, active, and obedient faith. The promise is that you will receive what God has promised; and what God has promised is deliverance in the Day of Judgment and eternal life—justification and eternal life. The relevance of this for justification is evident in the proof text the author chooses from the Old Testament. It is the same key proof text that the apostle Paul uses in Romans, namely, Habakkuk 2:3, 4. "My righteous one will live by faith." The "righteous one" is the one who perseveres in doing the will of God. He perseveres in an obedient faith. What he receives is what God has promised, and the promises of God are always received by faith. This righteous one does not survive the judgment by the merit of his works, but by faith, a faith that issues in faithfulness to the Lord.

Faith is expressly mentioned again in the final verse of the chapter, verse 39. "We are not of those who shrink back and are destroyed, but of those who believe and are saved." Those who will be justified and saved in the Day of Judgment are those who believe and who persevere in that faith. They persevere in doing the will of God. They persevere in faith, repentance, and obedience. In chapter 11 the author supplies a whole catalogue of such people. They are people who have believed the word of God, who have persevered in that faith and in doing the will of God. They will receive what was promised, but ultimately only in fellowship with us who are believers under the new covenant. They receive what was promised on the ground of what Jesus has accomplished for us by his death and resurrection. The message of Hebrews is that we who have believed in Jesus Christ as Lord and Savior, and who persevere in that faith in spite of the obstacles and opposition we meet along the way, will be justified and saved in the Day of Judgment. Therefore we should not grow weary, but "hang in there."

Assurance of Faith

These comments on perseverance lead naturally to a consideration of assurance. The exhortations to persevere in the Bible are often coupled with the promise of justification and eternal life. Hebrews 10:36 itself is a good example of this. "You need to persevere so that when you have done the will of God, you will receive what he has promised." James begins his letter in chapter 1 with an encouragement to persevere under many trials. These trials bring with them a temptation to be disobedient and to fall away from Christ (vs. 2–4). Over against this possibility of apostasy James says in verse 12, "Blessed is the man who perseveres under trial, because when he has stood the test, he will receive the crown of life that God has promised to those who love him." The man who perseveres is in the right with God. He is justified and he will

receive the crown of life. At the end of the letter James offers Job
as a prime example of one who has persevered in faith under great
trials and was blessed. God has promised to forgive our sins, to
renew us in the image of Christ, and to usher us into eternal life.
Scripture says that God will fulfill these promises. "You will receive
what he has promised" (Heb. 10:36). That is the foundation we
have for the assurance of our salvation in the Day of Judgment.

When we talk about justification we cannot avoid talking
about perseverance and we cannot avoid talking about assurance.
Assurance was really the issue for Martin Luther at the time of the
Protestant Reformation, and it became an issue for the Puritans
a century later. Can we have the assurance that we are justified
now in the sight of God and that we will be justified in the Day of
Judgment?

We can get at this matter of assurance by asking the question, When are we justified? Theologians have offered a variety of
answers to this question. Some say we are justified in the eternal
decree of God, and that this decree is simply worked out in the
course of history. Others say that we were justified when Jesus died
on the cross and rose again from the dead on the third day. That is
when our sins were atoned for, and so we were justified when Jesus
was justified as our sin bearer in his death and resurrection. Still
others say that we are justified at the moment when we are baptized, or at the moment when we come to personal faith in Jesus.
Then the justification that is prepared for us is made ours and we
are actually and personally justified. And then there are those who
say that we are justified really only in the final judgment.

There is a measure of truth in all of these views, but the key
to understanding the biblical doctrine lies in the last view mentioned. We will be justified on the day when we appear before the
judgment seat of Christ, and when each one will receive what is
due him for the things done while in the body, whether good or
bad (2 Cor. 5:10). Justification is a forensic act, that is, an act of
judgment. The final judgment is by pre-eminence the time when
God acts forensically in judgment, the time when God renders a
verdict that will never be appealed or reversed.

Jesus teaches in John 5 that the Father has given the Son of Man the authority to judge. At the general resurrection those who have done good will rise to live, and those who have done evil will rise to be condemned (v. 29). Jesus teaches that in the Day of Judgment he will require us to give an account of every careless word we have spoken. "By your words you will be acquitted (justified), and by your words you will be condemned" (Matt. 12:36, 37). In Acts 17:31, Paul says that God has set a day when he will judge the world with justice by the man he has appointed. In Romans 2 Paul speaks of a day to come when God will judge men's secrets and will give to each person according to what he has done. He says this in the context of his discussion of justification and condemnation. And as we have seen, James speaks of justification and condemnation as taking place in the Day of Judgment.

Now, again, the question of assurance is this, what is going to happen to me on that day, and can I know for sure what will happen to me? Is it possible to have assurance of my salvation from condemnation? The Roman church answered the Reformers by saying "No," because one never knows whether he will be in a state of grace at the hour of his death. The only exceptions are those who die by martyrdom and those who receive some special revelation from the Lord. The Puritans a century later also answered "No," unless you are assured by some unusual experience of grace (corresponding to Rome's idea of special revelation), or unless you have the works to prove that you are actually justified. They taught that we are justified by grace through faith alone, and not by works, but then proceeded to make works a basis for assurance. But just as we cannot be justified on the ground of our sin-stained works, so also we cannot really be assured on the ground of our sin-stained works. That is why assurance became as problematic for the Puritans as it was for Rome.

Over against this way of thinking the Reformers responded by affirming over against Rome, "Yes," we can know for sure what will happen to us in the Day of Judgment. We know by faith in Jesus Christ. Calvin and the Heidelberg Catechism actually go so far as to define justifying faith as "a deep-rooted assurance, . . . that

. . . I too, have had my sins forgiven, have been made forever right with God, and have been granted salvation" (Heid. Cat. Q. & A. 21). The basis for this assurance lies in the fact that 2,000 years ago Jesus passed through the final judgment for me and in my place. He died for my sin. In the space of three days he exhausted the penalty of eternal condemnation and then was raised from the dead. His own resurrection was his vindication, his justification, as the sin-bearer for his people. United to him by faith, I am justified in him. I do not have to wait until the final judgment to find out what will happen to me. I see in the resurrection of Christ what will happen. I know now what will happen to me in the Judgment because of what Jesus did for me 2,000 years ago in his death and resurrection. Because of what he did for me, I am now (presently) in a right relationship with God. I am right with God. That is to say, I am now justified and in a state of justification by faith in Jesus Christ. Jesus says in Luke 18 that the sinner went down to his house justified that very day (v. 14). He was justified in the day that he confessed his sin and begged for mercy. Paul says that Jesus was delivered over to death for our sins and was raised to life for our justification (Rom. 4:25). "Therefore, there is *now* no condemnation for those who are in Christ Jesus" (Rom. 8:1).

All these things are true: I was justified when Jesus died for me; I was justified when I was converted; I am now in a justified state; and I will be justified in the Day of Judgment. But it is precisely because of what will happen in the Day of Judgment that I can speak of a justification now, by faith. Justification as a present benefit in the application of redemption has meaning only because of what will happen in the Day of Judgment.

It is essential to note that this assurance is not simply information about the future and what is going to happen in the future. As believers we do not live by sight; we live by faith. It is the assurance that is given with faith in Jesus and faith in the promises that he has made to us. No one is privy to secret information about the future. No one can peer into the mind of God, or into his eternal decree. Assurance is the assurance that is given with faith in Jesus Christ. It is not an assurance that I have independently of my response to the gospel with a true and living faith. Therefore this assurance does not stay at the same level all the time. Faith can waver; it can be stronger or weaker at some times than it is at other times. Because obedience is the fruit of faith, my assurance will rise as I walk closer to the Lord in my love for him and surrender to his will. And because disobedience is the fruit of unbelief, my assurance will diminish as I wander away from the Lord in disobedience. We must cultivate assurance of grace and salvation in the same way that we cultivate faith, namely, by attention to the word of God, by the use of the sacraments that sign and seal the truth of that word, and by faithfulness to that word.

We have stressed the forensic character of justification. Justification is God's declaration that I am free from the guilt of sin, righteous in his sight, acceptable to him, and entitled to eternal life. Now when, where, and how does God make this declaration? Certainly he does so in the final judgment, and there he does so openly and publicly. We see that point illustrated in Matthew 25 where the Lord sits in judgment and separates the sheep from the goats. But just as the final judgment does not mean that I have to wait until that day to be justified, or to be assured of my justification, so also I do not have to wait until the final judgment to hear God's open and public declaration of justification and acceptance.

To make this point clear, I will compare it with a common understanding of what happens when the sinner is converted. A common understanding is that at the moment the sinner believes, God declares his justification in the courtroom of heaven. That is, God declares our justification in secret. This is when we are really justified—at the moment when we are converted. On the Day of Judgment God will simply announce openly and before a gathered humanity that once-for-all secret declaration. The judgment of the last day is therefore nothing more than a public announcement of a judgment that has taken place at another time and in another place and in total secrecy. Because it is so secret, no one can really know for sure that it has actually ever taken place at all.

The point to be made here is that the Bible knows nothing about a secret assize like the one just described. There is no secret courtroom where the sinner is not present to be judged, where he does not see the judge, and where neither he nor anyone else can hear this momentous ultimate judgment being pronounced. The Bible knows nothing of such a secret judgment. This secret judgment is a theological invention.

It is true that the judgment of the last day will be open and public. We will see the judge and we will hear his verdict. But even now in the course of our human experience the Lord pronounces his judgment, and we can hear it with our own ears. Even now he assures us of what will happen in the Day of Judgment so that we can know and have confidence in the midst of the challenges and trials of this life. And he does so again and again, openly and publicly, so that there will be no mistake.

This happens in the reading of God's word and in the preaching of his gospel when God's people are gathered before him to worship. The ordained minister whom we can see with our eyes represents to us the ministry of the ascended and ruling Christ himself. The pastor does not bring his own word from the pulpit, but the very word of God written down, and he proclaims that word to us. He tells us in the name of the triune God and with the authority of Christ that there is now no condemnation to those who are in Christ Jesus. He tells me that my sins are forgiven and that God has accepted me as his child. That is the good news of God's justifying verdict that I hear with my ears and receive by faith as the Holy Spirit drives that word home to my heart. The Lord then adds to the testimony of his word the testimony of the sacraments of baptism and the Lord's Supper. Both of these sacraments are from the Lord himself, and they are designed to confirm and strengthen our faith. They are designed to assure us that our sins are forgiven and that we have received the gift of eternal life because of the death and resurrection of Jesus.

Now, of course, there are many who hear that word of grace, that gospel, and they do not believe it. They do not believe what Christ is saying to them. They do not believe that Christ forgives sin or that their own sins are forgiven. They do not believe that they have sinned against the Lord, and therefore they do not repent of their sin or walk in the way of holiness. Some of these people are even in church every Sunday. If a sinner who hears the gospel does not embrace the forgiveness of sins promised to him there, he stands condemned. He has rejected the good news, and he will be condemned for his unbelief, his impenitence, rebellion, and disobedience. The gospel itself warns us about this awful possibility. The word of God tells us that the gospel is the aroma of life to some and the smell of death to others (2 Cor. 2:15). That is why the preaching of the gospel not only offers the promise of eternal life, calling us to faith and repentance, but also warns us of the terrible consequences of countering the gospel with unbelief.

Further, just as God's justifying declaration does not take place in secret, so also God's declaration of condemnation does not take place in secret so that the unbeliever cannot really be sure about what is going to happen to him on the day of judgment. Those who will be condemned for their unbelief and disobedience do not have to wait for the judgment day to hear God's verdict and what will happen to them. They hear God's verdict of condemnation when the whole gospel is preached including words of both gospel promise and gospel warning.

Paul describes ministers of the word as the ambassadors of Christ, as though God himself were making his appeal through them (2 Cor. 5:20). Jesus commissioned his disciples with these words, "Receive the Holy Spirit. If you forgive anyone his sins, they are forgiven; if you do not forgive them, they are not forgiven" (John 20:23). In his Commentary on John 20:23, after quoting 2 Corinthians 5:20, John Calvin writes,

> We now see the reason why Christ employs such magnificent terms, to commend and adorn that ministry which he bestows and enjoins on the Apostles. It is, that believers may be fully convinced, that what they hear concerning the forgiveness of sins is ratified, and may not less highly value the reconciliation which is offered by the voice of men, than if God himself stretched out his hand from heaven. And the Church daily receives the most abundant benefit from this doctrine, when it perceives that her pastors are divinely or-

dained to be sureties for eternal salvation, and that it must not go to a distance to seek the forgiveness of sins, which is committed to their trust.[1]

Those who minister in his name today minister with this same authority. They declare the sins of believers forgiven, and they hold unbelievers accountable for their sins. Again, ordained ministers do not do this on their own authority. Of course it is the Lord God alone who can forgive sin, and he reserves judgment to himself. But when pastors minister in the name of Christ and with the power of the Holy Spirit, the children of God hear the justifying verdict of their Father in heaven.

The bread and wine of the Lord's Supper confirm them in this knowledge because they are reminders of what Christ did for them 2,000 years ago. Thus they know what will happen to them in the Day of Judgment. Those who wrongly participate in unbelief are eating and drinking judgment to themselves. They know what will happen on the judgment day though they suppress that truth in unrighteousness (Rom. 1:18, 32). By eating and drinking at the table of the Lord, they are in effect acknowledging the rectitude of God's judgment unto condemnation. There is no *secret* assize before the Day of Judgment either for those who will be saved or for those who will be lost. By eating and drinking at the table of the Lord they are in effect acknowledging the rectitude of God's judgment.

We have now come full circle back to the question with which we began. The most practical and pressing theological question we can ask is this, What is going to happen to me in the Day of Judgment? The gospel is not nearly as complicated as we might think from looking at the many heavy tomes of scholastic theology written on the subject. We are justified and saved according to the eternal plan and purpose of God. We are justified in the death and resurrection of Christ 2,000 years ago. We are now justified by a living, active, penitent, and obedient faith in Jesus. And we are sure

1. John Calvin, *Commentary on the Gospel According to John*, trans. William Pringle (Grand Rapids, MI: Baker Book House, reprint 1979), 18:272.

to be justified when the ascended Christ returns to this earth to judge the living and the dead. That is the good news of the gospel, the gospel we believe and proclaim.

Norman Shepherd on Justification by Faith Alone: An Afterword

John H. Armstrong

When Professor Norman Shepherd was first challenged about his teaching on faith and repentance, back in the early 1980s, I was a complete outsider to the debate. The subsequent events that followed this time, many of which I now see as tragic for the church in general and some people in particular, provide a story in theological controversy and its aftermath. Much of what I heard, during the actual time of the so-called "Shepherd Controversy," came from Norm's critics, even from academics who asked to judge his work. It seemed to me, at least at the time, that he was denying justification by faith alone. This is what I was told, and I had no reason to believe otherwise. In particular it was said, in a suspicious manner, that he was denying a fundamental point made in the Westminster Confession of Faith, to which he had given subscription as a teacher at Westminster Seminary in Philadelphia. The sad tragedy is that Professor Shepherd was never tried, convicted or corrected in a proper manner. He was forced to undergo a theological trial *without a trial.* And he was encouraged to quietly leave his post, for the good of the school, while his critics would continue to attack him over the ensuing years.

As the years went by I continued to follow the various arguments that arose about the "Shepherd Controversy." There were several articles written and numerous comments were made in public and private. One student, at another seminary, even wrote a thesis about the "Shepherd Controversy," a work that I read. I listened carefully to the whole matter and sought to grasp what Norman was *really saying.* For some time I calmly assigned this whole episode to the category of "serious theological errors" made by good men who had to be challenged. I have since found that

such a conclusion is far too easy to make. This subject lent itself
to easy classification *without* the hard work required to understand
what Norman Shepherd was truly saying and not saying.

Some years later Norm became the pastor of a Christian
Reformed Church congregation in the Chicago area and began
to attend a ministerial fellowship that I moderated. This allowed
me to get to know him personally and to ask him a number of
questions. I saw the turn of his mind, the manner of his argu-
mentation and the way in which he so closely represented the rich
biblical theology of his own tutor, Professor John Murray, a man I
had long respected. Norm always responded with grace and wisdom. He never resorted to *ad hominem* attacks upon his opponents
and patiently listened to me as I worked through some of my own
questions and thoughts about the biblical text. I was profoundly
impressed.

Several years later, after engaging the Lordship controversies in general and then the growing debate over the language
of justification by faith alone in particular, I began to wonder if
Norman Shepherd might have been onto something that I had
badly missed. I found a set of theses that Norm had written during the controversy, theses which clearly laid out what he was saying and not saying. I read everything of Norm's I could find. I
then read, once again, the comments of his critics. I then decided
that it was time to sit down with Norm, along with several other
ministers, and discuss all of this. We asked a number of questions
and had a healthy discussion about biblical texts and theological
conclusions. I became convinced that Norman Shepherd was not
teaching a dangerous error. In fact, the opposite was the case. He
represented the very best of solid biblical theology *and* rightly em-
phasized faith and repentance in a Reformed way. It took me lon-
ger to become convinced that his views were within the boundaries
of the Westminster Confession, especially since I am not an expert
on the confession itself, but in time I came to believe that his view
grasped the statements of these esteemed writers quite faithfully.

Norman Shepherd's views had not changed at all. What
changed was my ability to listen to him and to consider carefully

what he was actually saying, and not saying, about faith, repentance, grace and works. In the smoke and fog of acrimonious debate I had allowed myself to be swayed by the views of some whom I respected. In the process I had not carefully read and thought about this subject for myself. I thus decided to seek Norm out once again. He was now living in professional retirement in Holland, Michigan. We talked, exchanged emails, met in private, etc. Patiently he answered my questions and therein pointed me to the authoritative Scripture with fresh insight and deep appreciation for the truth of the Word of God.

During this exchange I asked Norm if he had ever been given an opportunity to present his views on this controversial subject in one place where his thoughts about Scripture could be cogently argued and discussed by a gathering of church ministers and biblically earnest Christians. I was shocked to find out that this opportunity had never been afforded to him after more than 25 years! It seemed right that he should be given such an opportunity and that these proceedings should be taped, in both audio and video form. It also seemed right that he should be allowed to answer questions that arose in this setting. Further, I wanted some frontline biblical scholars to be in the room in order to interact with Norm and the audience cogently and critically. This led to a plan to host a Chicago Forum (2007), sponsored by the Center for Cultural Leadership (P. Andrew Sandlin) and ACT 3 (me) where this dialogue could happen over a three-day period. For those of us who were present, this time was immensely delightful, a positively enlightening time. Norm was gracious, as always, but he was challenged to explain his views and his teaching. Sadly, those who most disagree with him would not accept an invitation to attend or participate. I remain puzzled, and deeply saddened, by the way we conduct ourselves in theological debate and resolve to keep asking questions and learning all that I can to the end of my days.

The book that you hold in your hands comes from the (now edited) material that Norm presented in Chicago. By this means the teaching of Norman Shepherd can now be read and discussed in a much wider context. In addition, the audio and video presentations of this event are still available. Here you can see and hear what the whole event was really like. Questions are included on these presentations that are not in this book; thus those who would like to go further into this material, beyond the pages of the book, would benefit from these useful recordings. They are available to purchase as educational resources at: www.act3online.com or by calling (630) 221-1817.

My prayer is that many will come to appreciate the teaching of my dear friend and grow in the grace of Christ our Lord. To that end I happily encouraged and supported the printing of this material in this format. May the Father use it to speed a mighty reformation of biblical teaching about the free grace of God and the work of the Spirit in producing a life-transforming obedience of faith to Christ our Lord.

John H. Armstrong (B. A., M.A., Wheaton College; D. Min., Luther Rice Seminary) is president of ACT 3: Advancing the Christian Tradition in the Third Millennium, based in Carol Stream, Illinois. He is an adjunct professor of evangelism at Wheaton College Graduate School. He is a frequent guest on numerous radio programs, a contributing writer for several major periodicals and the author of hundreds of articles and essays. He is also the author/editor of eight books, the most recent being *Understanding Four Views of Baptism* (Zondervan, 2007). His new book, *Your Church Is Too Small* (Zondervan), will be released in the fall of 2009. John has been married for thirty-eight years and is the father of two married children and the grandfather of two.